10044689576840390171098102981056747859603987294857010910928091728394596079893475689
657100985768019284769102387650595997019810947596801984701817173968501985098284095867
97830198709698570126502860296870197810965496720198576039586174029509189203948503985
89105968701923046890987092019019280938570190818701948596948302910987079103920197210
40100980397391829039458687601948576940196857102939457106078192930123712987201987491
87869495801910291861542317561028457681928374978153938471928463747581928401010927472
576801949285069817263546757383838394771622112132101110871091821217145172748392091918172635472
20394801938475647382918001986069101918184019283746506819401948274859101989810123012
71019102919389475960101923627120302917302958375768910109998748576309281123413243132558697010
87840596879903456134318019837189101981714232413256079810109387685835243131234152408
57171624132419100010982837465192746573827619187620191982872635452987880019223762635
87678845553209090987312100912938817927576849301928758391097378909897091432543657659
765857680101981920919291827877665565655432090918909876767809093243234326547654980017
68172637261019201926871029495869109818372817509109687491870198209384768011254309891
59867092019586749381032958768793958671201918281910267654948572019384768473610101992
40978658967910928567849209184857601918101918386740987681019288746561019181759350110
591912431425398474650910198674839292837565637282976981726475869010101928388867592818
00191894598342537586940396748439311010198585776346352867509184768493483739209191980
58978717142321010199809184857687920918586740919386750191919858376091847567691019828
6091019860980910101019848678302981098009559687275869301987204958671019402918576019701
40197089101323142536596870187968701867794870596810193548675959876019785760196857010
30897013243565647656678940397879103869102435421756473546109309781021423451423615371
90909143542857684910927736457263540928766849587655467589765738976010909010924352616
68011223234132514352437658940398498578939586978102938594096857483958601232236455090
6857019132435407685940938576820191845746483939586748393029111423243546590798089706
51132430101922029370171615587968790385768209386879019287697089143526476809890985654
01982736540123546548302987394059687198576830191919135464537687980924351746583098675
58677980089714253022827263545069785712352536401983645201928756473465651423019093010
10958675840132435143245635768020909987685948476879709823647510131224253647798090809
79601142534465546352718298507698848201968750198698791010938572115243645362537465019
85968708901918918376453425342534096079857689405983726454132313231615371717283049170
11423100044758677980173645586779810958678790263748569273645473875201039182435243621
15333092758675648367409870898798011423356477059801982926354657856473647590182937480
15243546576893475865769019284657689038598216154233545152435698010198181827382716487
470990901524101119284635263748589769709887766463546576890382746586970181716253645673
1736454637281414142335353546576019191918181736475647564738290987182736475869876476891
27364501919181910292838475665768589494857683737485960119235494949596878694098123230
46354658677901910198273646578490192837465738392291782987000198282123411253546612379
47586970191817826354758687970898787654234756849348011323241323144657489687980098756
15243635463546697880991514235465748392010101919287465738382921098978797068796059090
14112435201010292838989890798756654534485768790152436128769584018364575888765465767
11000298791928374657576869797118191028374658677999920192837465738272615263748580098
14253001928485901524364758203910199902948576382919118273645001923893756676885848570
23100190929478566889991929384756890193847563827389509182873757889920394857665539201
16253233547586900198783748598697098776173643658019872766539480019876749869898101232
15243540019282736455657685903948572810191918283746575768798091131423352142353535008
26354637825342511010109125343520198287665435242534251526777019282773354647591010192
24354766587978980980909818763254467789901921837567483829847565342313243554657697012
15243364000199180001910293814141425364757680192837854758889901928785647388291010266
56516273658697091827364779101019287465748476391827364758901829837465789101928374611
51432536477890101992823734609991029283747281737466573483929019101818171413131225571
16125364019101001989283746575782091918727360100928757647869789910298172637465780107
16162542514200192874758690119101928374673827152635425163099289101918273636762532990
87871625344635271819991827366456734839290101019191234475674838291819190200142314262
154253620910192191817653465748348939384754759281773884656091839857648810298374651009
141310019289378675849110192827665634783831290098764893939001918181716263747587586904
14442536485768019187765655475668790001928726485901918187265444320101020291829847466
0909817256344565647484756688999987253546576586110191918127263553746578478578783011
09098253627172849585790101988778928819287463982767126651019282764657849837766101029
787846573820192837596978980899915243425166778201928374998898397657483201991010100924
78767171717272620202837465784997879011414142536270910910987655374658821019191783740
54635250001988775765748388872656475869018191827326364563728880019182736451019187268
25242435556709109109187654454678987654837657489092837464550918273645902917276552278
67671542435454657670101919101982747565867790182736455780192837589029877612534231243
24524524367567578909190198766847544657778810191992837475090908712123244550901817160
00191872625645657665789958677543427389099678908695847363010101928289291019387766589
78765432123455665430987909866778765412111219090876543456672727272746584867989884652
35460901928746579100987465761616253587690191877664857878785765652098765501019192993
78764556463756789987650981736455677388101918181891917848576879879874876397364593839
09094565432209876655498765789091019010197565765784839989891726354657010198782872760
57460191827666574087665424509871101918181716263647485769019191817163344401901901918
87654310910192828288151423423141142435620010191891826273645362701910901716151718182
56537374657687690189171514253646576870191827236356566778820101918172536475869780901
120987626234567485869701859384758690382736090890911312324354654767879801019141423354
13424353546576099101918191875768736465867791019102456786746353928275768798091827362
16276546478586970101019181726354546789098766654301911212132435452351515010101098899
13243650987899191919282374657686879719191917252453910101928586978090114253646573564

Title: *Conceptual Art*, 1989© [signature]

New York New Art

Meg Webster, *Moss Bed*, 1988, installation

Original Colour Graphic

KON-SU NAM

Conceptual Art, 1989©

An original colour graphic specially created for this issue by Kon-Su Nam. Conceived as a variation on the theme of numbers, the work is related to her painting of the same title.

Ross Bleckner, *Fallen Summer*, 1988, oil, 274.3 x 182.9 cm

An Art & Design Profile

New York New Art

David Salle, *Searching out Buddha*, 1986, acrylic and oil, 195 x 240 cm

ACADEMY EDITIONS • LONDON / ST. MARTIN'S PRESS • NEW YORK

Acknowledgements

This issue takes its theme from a series of major exhibitions in New York, including the Whitney Biennial, the Whitney Permanent Collection show and the Warhol Retrospective at The Museum of Modern Art, together with many other exhibitions which are credited individually throughout the issue. We are grateful to Kon-Su Nam for her invaluable contributions in compiling this issue.

Front Cover : Barbara Kruger, *Untitled* (Give me all you've got), colour photograph by Zindman/Fremont, courtesy Mary Boone Gallery; *Back Cover* : Leon Golub, *Two Black Men*, oil, courtesy the artist; *Inside Front Cover* : Doug & Mike Starn, *Triple Christ*, 1986, toned silver print with Scotch tape, aluminium, wood, glue and glass, courtesy John & Mable Ringling Museum, Sarasota, Florida; *Inside Back Cover* : Sol LeWitt Wall Drawings, 1989, installation, courtesy Kuntshalle Bern; *Half-Title* : Meg Webster, *Moss Bed*, installation, courtesy Whitney Museum; *Title Page* : David Salle, *Searching out Buddha, oil*, courtesy Leo Castelli Gallery; *Frontis* : Ross Bleckner, *Fallen Summer*, oil, courtesy Waddington Galleries; *Contents Page* : Frances Torres, *Oikonomos*, 1989, installation, *1989 Biennial Exhibition*, photo by Bill Jacobson courtesy Whitney Museum.

The Art of Quotation: An Interview with Robert Rosenblum
pp 6-17 : The following publications were useful in compiling the extended captions: Lita Barrie, 'Beyond the Looking Glass: Your Truths are Illusions', *Barbara Kruger*, National Art Gallery New Zealand, 1988; Dan Cameron, 'Signs of Empire', *NY Art Now: The Saatchi Collection*, London, 1987; Kim Levin, *Eric Fischl*, Saatchi Collection catalogue; Klaus Honnef, 'There is No Accounting for Taste', *Contemporary Art*, Taschen, 1988; Susan Krane, 'Art at the Edge', *Sherrie Levine*, High Museum of Art, Atlanta, Georgia, 1988. Illustrations courtesy the following: Barbara Kruger, courtesy the artist; Andy Warhol, Whitney Museum; Philip Taaffe and Peter Halley, Saatchi Collection; David Salle, Eric Fischl and Sherrie Levine, Mary Boone Gallery.

Cindy Sherman
pp 16-17 : Illustrations courtesy Saatchi Collection. This feature was compiled from the following essays: Craig Owens, 'The Discourse of Others: Feminists & Post-Modernism', *Postmodern Culture*, ed and intro Hal Foster, Pluto Press, London, 1985, p 75; Klaus Honnef, 'Staging Reality, or the Power of Photography', *Contemporary Art*, Tauschen, 1988, pp 208, 210.

Whitney Biennial
pp 18-23 : Kim Levin is a regular contributor to *Village Voice*, New York, where this essay first appeared. The extract and captions are taken from the Whitney catalogue *1989 Biennial Exhibition* and all illustrations are courtesy the Whitney Museum.

Kon-Su Nam
pp 24-29 : All illustrations were provided by the artist.

Leo Castelli: An Interview
pp 30-37 : Illustrations of work by Jasper Johns, Robert Rauschenberg, Frank Stella, Roy Lichtenstein, David Salle, Doug & Mike Starn and Robert Mapplethorpe courtesy Leo Castelli Gallery; Meyer Vaisman courtesy Saatchi Collection.

Pop Art II – Jeff Koons & Co
pp 38-45 : Illustrations courtesy the following: pp 38, 42, 43 and 44 courtesy Saatchi Collection; p 39 Sonnabend Gallery; p 41 Whitney Museum.

Donald Judd
pp 46-52 : Illustrations courtesy Waddington Galleries and the artist. The article on *Bilderstreit* is reproduced here as an edited version of the original text.

Nancy Spero
p 53 : Extracts by Jo-Anna Isaak and Robert Storr are taken from *Nancy Spero: Works Since 1950*, Everson Museum of Art, Syracuse, New York, 1984. Illustrations courtesy Everson Museum.

Leon Golub
pp 54-57 : This essay was first published in the exhibition catalogue *Leon Golub*, Barbara Gladstone Gallery New York. We would like to thank the author and gallery for allowing us to reproduce it here. Illustrations courtesy the artist.

Sol LeWitt
pp 58-59 : Sol LeWitt's Wall Drawings are reproduced here on the occasion of the exhibitions at Kuntshalle Bern and the Lisson Gallery London. Illustrations courtesy the artist.

Doug & Mike Starn
pp 60-61 : This extract was taken from *Doug and Mike Starn, The Christ Series*, John and Mable Ringling Museum of Art, Sarasota, Florida, 1988, with special thanks to Pat Buck. Illustrations courtesy the following: p 60, Saatchi Collection; p 61, Leo Castelli Gallery.

Exit Art, The Alternative Museum, Artist's Space
pp 62-67 : Exit Art: This feature was compiled from the organisers' statements; illustrations courtesy Exit Art. The Alternative Museum: This article was compiled from statements made in an interview between Gino Rodriguez and Roger Denson. Illustration courtesy The Alternative Museum. Artist's Space: This extract was taken from Linda Cathcart's introduction to *A Decade of New Art*, 1984. Works by Tim Rollins & KOS and Jonathan Kessler courtesy Saatchi Collection.

Julian Schnabel
pp 68-71 : Illustrations courtesy Pace Gallery and the artist.

Neo-Twilight: Ross Bleckner
pp 72-75 : Illustrations courtesy Waddington Galleries.

An Academy of Kitsch
pp 76-81 : Illustrations courtesy the following: Jeff Koons, Saatchi Collection; Jenny Holzer, the artist; Andy Warhol, Whitney Museum.

Bruce Nauman
pp 82-83 : Illustrations courtesy Saatchi Collection. *Bruce Nauman: Neons*, by Brenda Richardson, published by The Baltimore Museum of Art, 1983, was used in the preparation of this article.

American Art in the 20th Century
pp 84-96 : Works by Hartley, Bellows, Newman, Reinhardt, Stella, Johns, Serra, Warhol, Pearlstein, are courtesy the Whitney Museum. Works by Pollock, de Kooning, Twombly, Rosenquist are courtesy the Metropolitan Museum of Art. Both these publications were also useful in compiling extended captions. The work *Untitled*, by Mark Rothko is taken from the cover of the recent publication, Anna C Chave, *Mark Rothko: Subjects in Abstraction*, Yale University Press, New Haven, London, 1989.

Editor: Dr Andreas C Papadakis

First published in Great Britain in 1989 by *Art & Design*
an imprint of the
ACADEMY GROUP LTD, 7 HOLLAND STREET, LONDON W8 4NA
ISBN: 1-85490-004-8 (UK)

Art & Design Profile 16 is published as part of *Art & Design* Vol 5 7/8-1989
Published in the United States of America by
ST MARTIN'S PRESS, 175 FIFTH AVENUE, NEW YORK 10010
ISBN: 0-312-03976-X (USA)

Printed and bound in Singapore

Contents

Francesc Torres, *Oikonomos*, 1989, installation, *1989 Biennial Exhibition*, Whitney Museum

Barbara Kruger, *Above*: *Untitled* (A picture is worth more than a thousand words), 1987, colour photograph, 76 x 88 cm; *Below*: *Untitled* (You get away with murder), 1987, colour photograph, 76 x 76 cm. '. . . Kruger appropriates images from the media to expose the consumption of the cultural construction of "femininity". She mimics the graphic conventions which produce media stereotypes, but counters the immediate impact of the images with superimposed texts, subverting the underlying codes which dictate the "proper" reading. Through this disjunction of image and text, she exposes the cracks within the logic of advertising fictions to reveal how idealogical factors structure the unconscious mechanisms of viewing . . .' **Lita Barrie**

THE ART OF QUOTATION

An *Art & Design* Interview with Robert Rosenblum

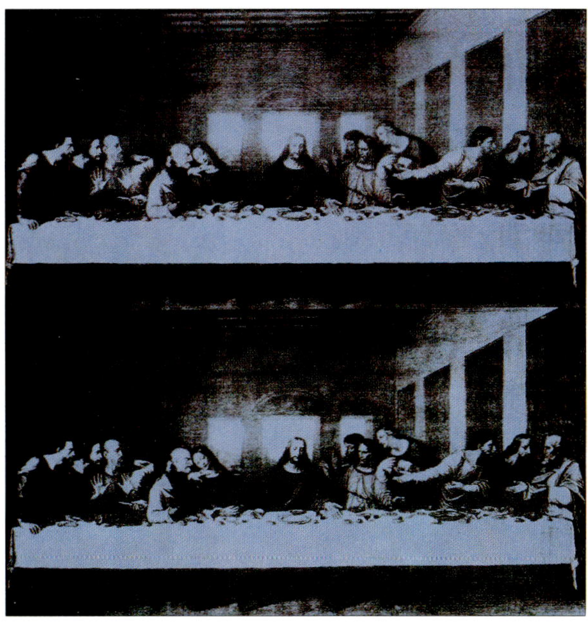

Andy Warhol, *Last Supper*, 1986, acrylic and liquitex, screenprint, 101.5 x 101.5 cm

From the 60s to the very last months of his life, Warhol's art, in fact, constantly intersected the major concerns of other artists – seniors, contemporaries, and juniors – casting its glance not only backward to the now remote world of Ad Reinhardt and Mark Rothko but forward to the most youthful activities of the 80s, from the making of art based on reproductions of reproductions, as in the work of Sherrie Levine or Mike Bidlo, to the bald use, in both two and three dimensions, of the most ordinary imagery and commodities from the world of commerce and advertising, as in the work of Jeff Koons of Haim Steinbach . . .

. . . Warhol figures large in the mood of the 80s, when the history of art, like the history of everything else, floats about in a disembodied public image-bank where Caravaggio and Schnabel can jostle for equal time in weekly magazines and daily conversations. In this context, Warhol is indispensable to an understanding of art about art, or the domain of what is called, more fancily, 'simulation' or 'appropriation' . . .

from 'Warhol as Art History'

– *In your essay for the catalogue of the MoMA retrospective, you discuss the influence of Warhol on the New York art world, the phenomenon of the artist as businessman and media figure, and the concept of art as a commercial product in a mass consumer market. Do you see Warhol as the most important influence on young artists working in New York today?*

Well I have to say that looking backwards I can think of no artist from the past 25 years who seems to have loomed so large as an ancestor figure, as the muse and guiding light of the younger generation, as Warhol; and my own sense – and this was in a strange way confirmed by the amount of exhibition space given to him at the Modern – is that he is, shall we say, for the last quarter century, what Picasso was to the first half of the 20th century. He seems to be everywhere and the potential of his art never seemed as huge as it suddenly did in the retrospective. So on every possible account he seems to be, for the moment, the great father figure.

– *In what way has Warhol's art had a visual impact on the work of younger artists?*

Well, in a strange way it probably had more of an impact in spirit than in visual fact, because one of the odd things about Warhol is that, at least on this side of the Atlantic and especially in New York, the actual work was very seldom exhibited. It's a kind of irony that in spite of his international fame, there has not been a proper Warhol retrospective in New York City since the early 70s. So for an entire younger generation, his art was virtually invisible, except of course in reproduction and in terms of its myth-making capacity.

– *Have there been any major revelations about his art for the younger generation of artists?*

One of the great revelations was to do with a supplementary show which we had at New York University, which was shown at the same time as the major retrospective and which concentrated exclusively on his work of the 50s – a whole decade of Warhol when he was a very successful commercial artist. I compare this – though I'm sure a lot of people would think it blasphemy – to the *Early Cézanne* show in so far as it disclosed a whole premature decade of activity which, once seen, changed for ever our perception of what was to come. For instance, there's a prevailing myth that Warhol virtually began from scratch around 1960-61 as a grass-roots artist who did very coarse, ugly, 'bottom of the social ladder' imagery – New York coast headlines, that sort of thing. In fact, as the exhibition here proved, in that decade he was working, among other things, in high style

Philip Taaffe, *South Ferry*, 1985/6, linoprint collage, acrylic, 110 x 95 cm. 'Places are continually being changed; one position is usurped by another position – and this is pretended to be an almost infinite progression. But we've learned in recent years not to trust these kinds of developments . . . We have to re-identify what the goals of modernism have become . . . Certainly, as usual, there's a crisis of faith. And faith as a category of psychological meaning is something we need to address. It's important to determine the ways in which our belief has failed us. How are we to re-channel our miscast belief? How do we make the leap from modernist faith to a faith in what has supplanted modernism?' **Taaffe, from an interview with Dan Cameron, *NY Art Now***

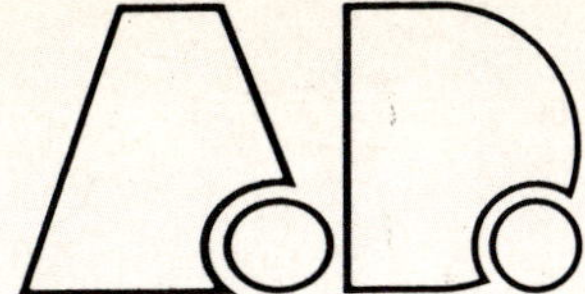

Art & Design

'The Art Magazine for the 80s'

Art & Design has quickly established a reputation for its influential, in-depth coverage of painting, sculpture and design. Always visually stunning, it takes its themes from current exhibitions or newly emergent trends, and gives its own fresh, thought-provoking angle on issues central to the art of today with articles by an international forum of critics, including Mary Rose Beaumont, Richard Cork, John Griffiths, Marco Livingstone and Robert Rosenblum.

An annual subscription for six double issues of *Art & Design*, including p&p, costs £35.00 in the UK, £39.50 in Europe, and US$75.00 or the sterling equivalent overseas.

A combined subscription for *Art & Design* and *Architectural Design*, giving six double issues of both magazines inclusive of p&p, is also available at the annual rate of £65.00 in the UK, £75.00 in Europe, and US$135.00 or the sterling equivalent overseas. On both the individual and combined subscriptions, students are entitled to a discount.

Individual issues can be ordered by mail for £7.95/US$19.95 + £1.00/US$3.00 (including p&p).

Recent and forthcoming issues:-

1/2-87	20th-Century British Art
3/4-87	The Post-Modern Object
5/6-87	Abstract Art
7/8-87	The Post-Avant-Garde
9/10-87	British & American Art
11/12-87	Sculpture Today
1/2-88	David Hockney
3/4-88	The New Modernism
5/6-88	The Classical Sensibility
7/8-88	Art in the Age of Pluralism
9/10-88	British Art Now
11/12-88	The New Romantics
1/2-89	Italian Art
3/4-89	40 Under 40
5/6-89	Malevich
7/8-89	New York, New Art

Subscriptions Department
ACADEMY GROUP LTD
7/8 Holland Street
London W8 4NA
Tel: 01-402 2141

All major credit cards accepted

ART & DESIGN MAGAZINE SUBSCRIPTION

Please send me one year's subscription to Art & Design

Full rate UK £35.00 Europe £39.50 Overseas US$75.00 **Students** UK £29.50 Europe £34.00 Overseas US$65.00

☐ **Payment enclosed by cheque/postal order/draft**

☐ **Please charge £ . . . . . to my credit card account no:**

Expiry date . . . .

Signature ....

Name ....

Address..

....

....

Subscriptions Department
ACADEMY GROUP LTD
7/8 Holland Street
LONDON W8 4NA

ARCHITECTURAL DESIGN + ART & DESIGN

Please send me one year's subscription to both magazines

Special introductory combined rate UK £65.00 Europe £75.00 Overseas US$135.00
Special introductory student rate UK £59.50 Europe £69.50 Overseas US$120.00

☐ **Payment enclosed by cheque/postal order/draft**

☐ **Please charge £ . . . . . to my credit card account no:**

Expiry date . . . .

Signature ....

Name ....

Address..

....

....

Subscriptions Department
ACADEMY GROUP LTD
7/8 Holland Street
LONDON W8 4NA

ARCHITECTURAL DESIGN MAGAZINE

Please send me one year's subscription to Architectural Design

Full rate UK £45.00 Europe £55.00 Overseas US$99.50 Students UK £39.50 Europe £49.50 Overseas US$89.50

☐ **Payment enclosed by cheque/postal order/draft**

☐ **Please charge my credit card account no:** (all major cards accepted)

Expiry date ....

Signature ....
Name ....
Address..
....
....

Subscriptions Department
ACADEMY GROUP LTD
7/8 Holland Street
LONDON W8 4NA

Architectural Design

Architectural Design continues its tradition of vigorous and wide-ranging treatment of architectural trends of vital importance to today. The issues, which are published six times a year on alternate months, are each devoted to a major theme of topical relevance. Leading architects to be featured in 1989 include Peter Eisenman, Michael Graves, Zaha Hadid, Hans Hollein, Arata Isozaki, Charles Jencks, Leon Krier, Daniel Libeskind, Richard Meier, Cesar Pelli, Aldo Rossi, Denise Scott Brown, James Stirling, Bernard Tschumi and SITE.

An annual subscription for *Architectural Design*, including postage and packing, costs £45.00 in the UK, £55.00 in Europe, US$99.50 or the sterling equivalent overseas.

A combined subscription for *Architectural Design* and *Art & Design*, giving six double issues of both magazines inclusive of postage and packing, is also available at the special introductory annual rate of £65.00 in the UK, £75.00 in Europe, and US$135.00 or the sterling equivalent overseas.

For both the individual and combined subscriptions, students are entitled to a discount.

Individual issues can be ordered by mail at a cost of £7.95/US$19.95 + £1.00/US$3.00 postage and packing per issue.

Please complete the subscription form opposite and send it with your payment
NOW

Subscriptions Department
ACADEMY GROUP LTD
7/8 Holland Street
London W8 4NA
Tel: 01-402 2141

All major credit cards accepted

Peter Halley, *White Cell with Conduit*, 1986, acrylic, day-glo and roll-a-tex, 147.5 x 285 cm. 'In my recent critical writing, I have been very much involved with the idea of revising some of the categories of experience we're used to dealing with, like nature, and more specifically death . . . I've replaced these ideas with what I call hyper-realisation: as one generation of art follows the next, the present takes immediate past, assigns it the value of the real, and then says it's going to take it a step past the real, in terms of abstraction or formal emptying. I'm very involved with this model of hyper-realisation in terms of the constant renovation of modernism, which I prefer to the death metaphor.' **Halley, from an interview with Dan Cameron, *NY Art Now***

commercial art – he worked with Tiffany's and so on – and was completely immersed in the fusion of art, commerce and advertising in a way that suggests that his choice of low-down imagery and, in the course of time, of commercial illustration, was a very conscious and sophisticated one. So it was not a question of someone at the bottom of the social and economic ladder starting at rung one, but rather somebody who had, in a very wilful and elegant way, chosen to descend from the top. I would also say about The Museum of Modern Art retrospective, in addition to showing us acres of work from the 60s and 70s that we had never properly seen in New York or seen at all, it was, at least for me, something of a revelation in terms of the very late works. My own sense was that the late work was under-exhibited in much the same way as the late work of Picasso was.

– *Why do you think that was?*

I think there are several reasons: one is that, in order to show it in proper quantity and give it a fair spread, it simply would have taken up too much room – many of the late paintings are absolutely huge; for example, a proper display of the variations of *The Last Supper* and works like those would have taken practically an entire museum. And, I suppose, given a choice of having a full representation of the serial pictures of the 60s or the work of the last four or five years, they chose the former.

– *You talk about Warhol's late works in which he is quoting from art history – from Leonardo, Munch, De Chirico etc – as intersecting the interests of younger artists. Do you think these artists were actually influenced by Warhol?*

I don't think so. I think it's more a question of *zeitgeist*, because my own guess – it's almost more than a guess – is that very few younger artists, at least in New York, were aware of these Warhol works about other works of art. He did for instance have an exhibition of late De Chirico phrasings, quotations after quotations; but it was amazing to me how little attention it was given – nobody seemed to have gone to see it or to talk about it – and my own hunch is that if you had asked most savvy New York people five years ago about Andy Warhol and Munch they would never have known that he had done works after Munch. So all of this was a kind of underground activity and when it was exposed, really for the first time, it was a kind of 'eureka' sensation that he clicked into place. I think what we ought to emphasise sufficiently is how invisible Warhol has been in New York over the last ten years or so, he has just never been given a fair shake.

Eric Fischl, *Bayonne*, 1985, oil, 259.1 x 327.7 cm.'Fischl is usually grouped with the new breed of so-called Neo-Expressionist artists. Rejecting abstract modernist ideas and ideals, and the objectivity of minimalism and photo-realism . . . "You were to invent a new world, but you weren't given any skills to do it." . . . The figures he paints are often inexplicably nude. He presents them as exhibitionists and makes us into voyeurs, implicating them and us in surreptitious exploits and exploitations . . . "One, truly, does not know how to act! Each new event is a crisis, and each crisis is a confrontation that fills us with much the same anxiety that we feel when, in a dream, we discover ourselves naked in public." '
Kim Levin

David Salle, *Coming and Going*, 1987, acrylic, oil and photosensitised linen on canvas, 243.8 x 339.1 cm. Salle 'uses pornographic magazines as well as highly meaningful but encoded paintings from serious art . . . He projects the various subjects on top of one another . . . His paintings are a symptomatic illustration of the bewildering visual repertoire of modern man and modern civilisation . . . The structure of his paintings is extremely complex – a reflection, as it were, of the complex appearances of our world, where ideas and mental images, once they have become visual, are considered to be just as real as the phenomena which are physically tangible or can be experienced psychologically.'
Klauss Honnef

– What impact do you think Warhol has had on the nature of the art world in New York? His statement, 'Being good at business is the most fascinating kind of art', seems to have particular relevance to today's artists.

Yes, I think the spirit of Warhol, which may have started in a kind of mock ironic way in the early 60s, has really replaced in a fully-fledged way the earlier mythology of the artist as being totally uninterested in the perhaps almost hostile world of money, bourgeois values and so on. I would say that this is a myth like the previous one and has just totally turned that one upside down. But as we all know from the late 19th century, right through the 1940s, 50s and 60s, people had the idea, and artists had the idea, that art ought to be a kind of taking of vows; that if you were going to be an artist, it was a fact that you were not interested in material values, you rejected the world of commerce, the world of middle-class pleasures and so on. This was obviously a very fertile myth and many people have lived by it; the Abstract Expressionists in New York were probably the last gasp of faith in that sanctity of art and the feeling that it had nothing to do with the here and now of commerce and materialism of our society. But that myth seemed to have become pretty silly or moribund by the 1960s with the Pop generation, and Warhol was probably the strongest and earliest voice to deflate it. Now I think the prevailing myth, the prevailing fantasies about art, is that art is business like everything else, it's like fashion or entertainment; there's absolutely no reason why artists should have this 'holier than thou' attitude towards what they do.

– Does this mean that the public in New York now sees art purely in terms of fashion and entertainment, rather than in more serious terms as a form of aesthetic or social critique?

I think it's absolutely true that the atmosphere, especially in New York, about going to openings of art exhibitions, museums, retrospectives, even just symposia discussions, all of this has the flavour of carnival, of fun culture, high society. It has to do with the sense of esteem that one can have by being associated with the most current trends of the art world; it's very equatable with the world of fashion and high style and all this has permeated the thinking as well as the look of young artists.

– But do you think this has had a negative effect on the quality of the art?

No. My own sense is that in terms of the mythologies – the cultural support for works of art – I don't think it makes very much difference one way or another about good or bad because my own feeling is that throughout history, at any given time there are a handful of really terrific artists. There have been many periods in the history of Western art in which the prevailing myths or things that create art have been absolutely obnoxious, but great art has been produced. What I'm simply saying is that art and the cultural myths that have exploded are not identical and I've seen terrific works of art from the 1980s that may be about art as a commodity but that doesn't mean that the concept of art as a commodity is good or bad; rather it has to do with the quality of the art itself.

– Some critics have seen artists as merely responding to the demands of the New York art market, the pressure from dealers to come up with new gimmicks that may last for only one season, raising the artist to instant commercial success, only to be replaced the following season by yet another, more commercially viable product.

I think that's probably true. I would say that the tempo of change and also the tempo of interest and curiosity about new works of art may be greater now than it has ever been in the past. I always find it a little heartbreaking for example that artists whom I myself have been very enthusiastic about, I've then totally forgotten about because they've been instantly replaced by somebody else who fills the screen. I think this may get sorted out, it may just be the phenomenon of being in the present. Looking back on the 60s for example, the tempo of change also seemed to be very rapid. It may just be that now the present is coming up with such rapidity that things can't stand out.

– Frederic Jameson has used the phrase 'the perpetual present' in relation to the tempo of the art world in New York; and philosophers such as Jean Baudrillard have seen the influence of the media, particularly of television, as having had a significant impact on the work of younger artists and on the visual demands of the market. Do you think this is true?

Well I think it's true, but it should also be said that a 'perpetual present' also involves a 'perpetual past', because one of the characteristics of our perpetual present is to be endlessly curious in terms of resurrecting, re-examining works from decades ago; and the market, it seems to me, and our ability to get sated is such that people are always looking for more and more and more to see, to re-examine, to buy. And it's not only a question of younger artists but also of older artists; it's rather amazing for example how many revivals there have been of art of the 50s, the 60s, the 70s – the museums are doing it all the time. So it's not just a question of being interested in the new and the young, but of being interested in everything, so that excavation of the recent historical past is greater than it's ever been.

– In your essay you discuss the idea of 'excavating memories', of quoting from art history. Do you see this as the most significant tendency in Post-Modern art of the late 80s, and how is this tendency reflected in the work of young artists?

Well there is throughout the work of the 80s the most extraordinary self-consciousness of earlier works of art. This is, as everybody knows, a period of acute awareness of art history, we see it all the time in magazines, newspapers, exhibitions and the glut of reproductions. You will note that artists today are always quoting from other works of art, sometimes in terms of drawings after famous earlier works; for example both David Salle and Julian Schnabel look back to the work of old masters – you will find quotations from Watteau, Caravaggio, Gericault in their work. Other artists seem to be exclusively concerned with the pantheon of 20th-century high art, so that artists like Mike Bidlo or Sherrie Levine do virtually exact replications of works by Picasso or Brancusi. But the sense of the visual data-bank of art history has almost turned into nature in terms of the experience of the late 20th century, as landscape was in the 19th century. It's the reality that we pick and choose from, it comes in all kinds of variations and combinations, and it makes perfect sense; I mean when you see people walking around with shopping-bags that have Renoir pictures on them, or pictures by Warhol (even more appropriate), its a form of advertising culture that proves that art is reflective.

– Some critics have seen the current tendency of quoting from art history in a negative light, as implying a lack of originality in the minds of young artists. Do you think this is a fair criticism?

I don't think it's any more of a lack of originality than sitting down and copying nature, for example a still life. The whole idea of art as copying something that already exists is deeply ingrained in Western tradition and what's original about it is the way in which it is translated into something new that you can see. So I don't think on principle anything is more original than anything else.

– Do you see the art of quotation as playing a predominant role in the 80s debate on how to reintroduce subject matter after decades of Modernism and absolute abstraction?

Yes, I think that this is a very important revolution and it's one that began and should be pinpointed in the work of Andy Warhol and also in the art of Rauschenberg. The point is that after what at least from the New York vantage point seemed to be like an

SHERRIE LEVINE

'Sherrie Levine's work vies for position among the most hotly debated art of this decade . . .

. . . Through her art Levine exaggerated and symbolised what Baudrillard termed today's state of "hyperreality" – a condition that negates the possibility of genuinely experiencing "reality" in a culture where all objects, images, and reactions have been preprocessed for us and capitalised on through the very modes of their public presentation. Levine's appropriations . . . amplify this notion that the effect and the importance of an object in the later 20th century (with its perhaps debased fin-de-siècle air) is largely determined and propelled by the market rather than by intrinsic values . . .

> The world is filled to suffocating. Man has placed his token on every stone. Every word, every image, is leased and mortgaged. We know that a picture is but a space in which a variety of images, none of them original, blend and clash. A picture is a tissue of quotations drawn from the innumerable centers of culture. . .We can only imitate a gesture that is always anterior, never original. Succeeding the painter, the plagiarist no longer bears within him passions, humours, feelings, impressions, but rather this immense encyclopedia from which he draws. The viewer is the tablet on which all the quotations that make up a painting are inscribed without any of them being lost. A painting's meaning lies not in its origin, but in its destination. The birth of the viewer must be at the cost of the painter.

Untitled (Double Lead Checks: 8), 1988, casein/lead, 101.6 x 50.8 cm

In the terms of Roland Barthes (who, along with Franz Marc, Levine paraphrased in the above "artist's statement"), her art assumes the position of a "text" to be read and to extend allegorically. It is constructed to reveal strata of thought: as such it stands in distinction to a clearly defined, insular "work". Levine's recent paintings . . . purposely confuse the issue. They are referential and rhetorical "texts", yet they are asserted as visually potent objects in and of themselves, mimetic as they may be. They again reveal the hand – "the inscription" – of their author, assumed to be denied by her procedures.

The series of lead checks and knot paintings embody contradictions and oppositions. They evince an involuted way out of the deadened dilemma of modernism's linearity – an endpoint recognised and reckoned with by artists as diverse as Malevich, the Dadaists, Mondrian and Duchamp.'

Susan Krane

eternal take-over of modern art by the abstract painters of the 40s and 50s – I mean that was what art meant in the 50s, Abstraction and Abstract Expressionism – the next problem was how to reintroduce legible things that we can all recognise from the world around us. What artists like Rauschenberg and above all Warhol did was to reintroduce this kind of familiar imagery, not by copying it in the conventional pre-abstract way, but by using second-hand reproductions – namely photographs or comic strips, all of these translated into among other things silk-screen prints, so that we began to look at these reproductions of reproductions, that surprising and stealthy way in which reality was reintroduced in the 60s. Warhol really is in the dead centre of this; he preferred for example to project images of tragedy, of horror in his American disasters, not through painted copies of electric chairs but through photographs of them. And all of this mutation of second-degree imagery, images after images, is deeply ingrained in the experience of life as well as art of the last 30 years or so.

– *How do you see this tendency towards reproductions of reproductions emerging in the art of the late 80s?*

In every possible way. I think the most extreme statement of it, one could say the purest statement of it, is in the work of Mike Bidlo, namely an artist who tries to make exact facsimiles of existing works of art, usually working after reproductions after the original because it is after all mainly through reproductions that we know these works. That is the most extreme possibility.

– *Would you describe this type of art in terms of* critical *appropriation, or simply as art about art? What are the ideas behind Bidlo's reproductions, and those of other contemporary artists?*

I think in his particular case there are any number of reasons for an artist making an exact copy of a work of art, it's part of the whole tradition of passing on famous icons of the past into the present, as art has done throughout history: for example Rubens copied Leonardo and Gericault copied Caravaggio and so on. In Bidlo's particular case however, it seems to be respectful, there's this feeling of awe about these masterpieces from the first part of the 20th century, which for younger artists seem to be so far away that they could have existed in the 5th century BC; they are handing on values and to replicate them is a worshipful act of veneration, or so it seems to me. That is one aspect of it. In Bidlo's case they are not made by machine, they are hand-made and lovingly detailed and they try to mimic the actual touch of the artist; but they are also, on a more lofty conceptual level, about art as replication, they are pictures that have to do with the age of reproduction. One of the fascinating things for instance you can find these days is how many different variations there are on *Les Demoiselles d'Avignon* – the picture seems to loom so large as a historical cult painting, it is generally considered to be a quantum leap into the 20th-century. Any number of artists have done variations on it, sometimes satirising it. I can think of a wonderful example by the black artist Robert Colescott called the *Demoiselles d'Alabama*. He shows the five Picasso prostitutes as rather hot ladies of the American South – that's one way to do it! Picasso of course did his own appropriation, copied it and varied it himself in his late work; Mike Bidlo just copies it pure. But one could pick up on any number of masterpieces and the various ways in which they have been repeated. But now that I've said it, while all this seems so new and distinctive to the 1980s, it is perhaps not so new when one thinks for example of the 19th century and the early 20th – one can think of any number of masterpieces from the past that have been treated with the same kind of veneration, such as Velasquez's *Las Meninas* which has been copied in various permutations and combinations throughout the late 19th century and early 20th century. It's like all new things which seem so new, when the dust settles they may seem part of a far longer, grander tradition.

– *Appropriation or pastiche is also discussed in relation to abstract art in the 80s, the so-called 'Neo-Geo' artists such as Peter Halley, Philip Taaffe, Peter Schuyff, Sherrie Levine etc. Their work has been criticised as derivative, repetitive, superficial, meaningless and market-oriented. How do you view their art in the context of current New York trends?*

I am interested in a lot of these abstract artists, including Peter Halley and Peter Schuyff. One of the things I enjoy about them is the degree of absolute fragidity in their work; they all seem to be hell-bent to make pictures that are so tough, so cold, so unfeeling that you might think a robot or a computer was responsible for them. It seems to me that the new emotional experience is something that has to do with feeling a new range of sub-zero temperature, that is how cold can you get, how completely impersonal, how chilly and computer-like can you be. And it's funny, it has to do with certain literary counterparts of fictional deadpan description; you sense different ranges of temperature, of wilful lack of feeling and it turns sort of inside out, upside down; it's a coldness that is so cold that it becomes exciting in itself. Actually when I think about it, this is a kind of complaint that used to be levelled against artists like Mondrian who were considered to be absolutely unfeeling, cerebral, chilly, no emotions and so on; nobody says that anymore and I think the same thing is going to happen to these artists. For the moment a lot of people accuse them of looking as if they were robots rather than feeling painters but I think that their range of emotions will become far more visible, more sensible in years to come.

– *Would you say that their work evolved primarily as a reaction to the Neo-Expressionist paintings of the early 80s?*

Yes very much so because there seemed, especially after the 1970s which were so dominated by cerebration, to be this absolute volcano of personal liberation, as if every artist's *id* had exploded; there was the most free-exploding world of fantasy images coming from both sides of the Atlantic, sometimes terrific, sometimes boring, as is always the case in any range of artists. I think this coldhearted calculation is a kind of check, and also in a fascinating way, as in the case of Philip Taaffe, it has to do with permutation once again. His pictures very often take the classics of the 1950s, works say by Barnett Newman and Bridget Riley, and put them into a deep computer freeze. So it's as if some electronic artist had metamorphosed the impersonal look of Bridget Riley onto another level of fragidity. These artists of the 1980s are thus quoting in various degrees of seriousness or irony the art of the 1950s and before; and it is now clear that the whole history of Modernism is something that is completely in the past tense and has to be looked at from a completely new angle.

– *Do you see then the art of Neo-Expressionism as looking more towards the future in the sense that it was conceived as a definite reaction to Modernism and a return to figurative art?*

Everything that is new looks towards the future, even if it is nominally looking at the past; although one of the things I must say about these Neo-Expressionists is that they too have this retrospective character – I'm thinking particularly about the German painters such as Baselitz or Rainer Fetting, who quite consciously look back to the Expressionists of the early part of 20th century, Nolde, Kirchner and so on. So that their Expressionism is very much 'neo' in the same way that when Peter Halley does Barnett Newman again he's 'neo', but they're just as much a part of this looking backwards to the Modernist past as the abstract painters of the Neo-Geo movement.

– *How do you regard the controversial figure of Julian Schnabel, both in terms of Neo-Expressionist painting and in the context of the contemporary art world of New York as a whole?*

Schnabel seems to me rather fascinating as an artist who is trying to be as it were a neo-mythological hero of modern art. I think he built up a programme and a look for himself that would revive the whole sense of greatness and grandeur of the macho artist in his studio attacking the world. I think he thought of himself as a neo-Picasso and there is something second-degree about this too, it's theatrical and it's almost another example of the role-playing, the retrospective role-playing that we've seen so often in the 80s.

– *How does the art of Eric Fischl and David Salle fit into the context of this retrospective painting of the late 80s?*

Fischl and Salle are both artists I like immensely for different reasons. Fischl I must say seems very off-beat in terms of artists of the 1980s. One of the reasons is that at least in his earlier works he seemed to be so absolutely unsophisticated in terms of just recording like a photographer the facts of American upper middle-class life, which was a kind of programme that no other artist I can think of took on. His work has covered a whole range of experience that seemed absolutely impossible for high style painting to any other artist – I don't know how he ever dreamed up the possibility of doing it or imagined transcribing it. For me, he put his finger on the pulse of modern America in a way that is absolutely miraculous. The only painter I can compare him to is Edward Hopper who managed to translate into visual terms what must have been the feel of America in the 1920s, 30s and 40s; and it would seem to me that for 21st-century sociologists or historians, if they want to find out the way a good section of American life looked and felt and meant in the 1980s, they could do no better than to turn to Eric Fischl's work.

– *Do you see Fischl then as less retrospective than other artists working in New York?*

Yes, in that way he seems to be most concerned with recording directly current events, which as a rule he takes from the model or, if he works from photographs, he paints in an earlier first-hand way. On the other hand, one of the odd ironies of this is that even though it seems to be direct pictorial experience, it is the kind of work – I just mentioned Hopper before – that summons up a long genealogical table in terms of the history of American realist art. For one thing it very wilfully evokes some images like those of Winslow Homer, an artist who looms large in terms of American parochial history – national history – but who may seem very secondary in terms of International Modernism. But Fischl has in some way looked backwards to this realist tradition

BARBARA KRUGER

'Just as Kruger's work blurs the distinction between art and media, it also blurs the distinction between art and theory. The theory at issue is post-structuralism, based on the premise that the world is experienced as a vast text through which we see ourselves. The aim of feminist theory is to rewrite the text which constructs our psyches. Kruger's work takes its impetus from Jacques Derrida's strategy of "deconstruction", which aims to displace patriarchal binary oppositions to re-inscribe them with different meanings. In Kruger's work the displaced oppositions are: identity/difference, subject/object, surveyor/surveyed, prowess/pose, active/passive, culture/nature, history/fiction, based on the opposition man/woman, which she emphasises with the shifting pronouns, You/I , They/We . . .

Kruger plays upon the linguistic nature of images as visual texts which read (**A picture is worth more than a thousand words).** Advertising and the media use superimposed texts to fix and regulate the reading of an image . . .

Kruger stages a critique of the capitalist manipulation of art (particularly her own work) within New York's hard-sell, consumer-orientated Mary Boone Gallery. The notoriety of this gallery is based on the manufacturing of male artists (notably Julian Schnabel and David Salle) into media superstars . . . [who] merely revamp old art-referential genres to proclaim the pedigree of their work as collectible art. In contrast, Kruger's work . . . attempts to place art within its cultural context, as social signs existing alongside other social signs in order to disrupt repressive cultural codes . . .

It is perhaps the final irony of Kruger's interventionist approach that she should enter the predominantly male 'stable' of a gallery which perpetuates the mythical status of artists whose work is based on humanist fictions of an essential self-hood. Kruger's work deconstructs these fictions by exposing the processes through which subjectivity is shaped, formed and positioned within language and images . . .

Kruger uses an image of a tray of chocolates inside a pink frame to mime a conventional ploy of male sexual propositioning . . . [and] reverses the positions in this power relationship by quoting the cliché . . . **Give me all you've got –** in a feminine demand for money and sexual pleasure.'

Lita Barrie

Untitled (Give me all you've got), 1987, colour photograph, 122 x 152 cm

which was pretty much ignored by most ambitious artists from the 1950s on. So in this unexpected way he might be said to participate in this looking backwards mood of our time. But his subject matter is certainly unique and just extraordinarily valuable it seems to me because he has managed to produce images that people in America recognise instantly; it's that marvellous feeling as in reading a novel that you're so glad that somebody else has described it because nobody's ever done it before.

– *How does the art of David Salle compare to that of Fischl? Does he succeed likewise in producing images that communicate with the viewer on a level of common recognition?*

David Salle is a quite different sort of artist and would certainly be a central figure in any discussion of art of the 1980s, not only from the level of appropriation – quotations from artists from a range of earlier art history – but above all in terms of the collision, the juxtaposition, of completely disparate images. It's become an absolute cliché in the 80s to talk about this mirage of multiple, contradictory images experienced in everyday life, and I guess the architype of this is our television sets on which we just switch channels. But in any case, it may be a platitude, but it's simply also a fact of the way we live now and David Salle with his silk-screen effects and his constant jarring – everything from abstract textural designs, of fabrics and so on, to academic drawings of nudes, side by side – is very much a part of the facts of visual life today and he has pinpointed that in a very personal style. Once again, like everything else, it may seem very new, but in retrospect any number of distinguished ancestral roots come to mind; for instance it very much recalls the split-screen imagery of James Rosenquist. Likewise the large scale is very American in quality and is one of the things that gives David Salle his touch, I mean it's the hugeness of his imagery, which was something that was established in the 60s by Rosenquist and of course the whole tradition of Rauschenberg; this is very much a part of the background to Salle. He's just retranslated it into a very fresh and 1980s look that seems to reflect the mood of the television generation.

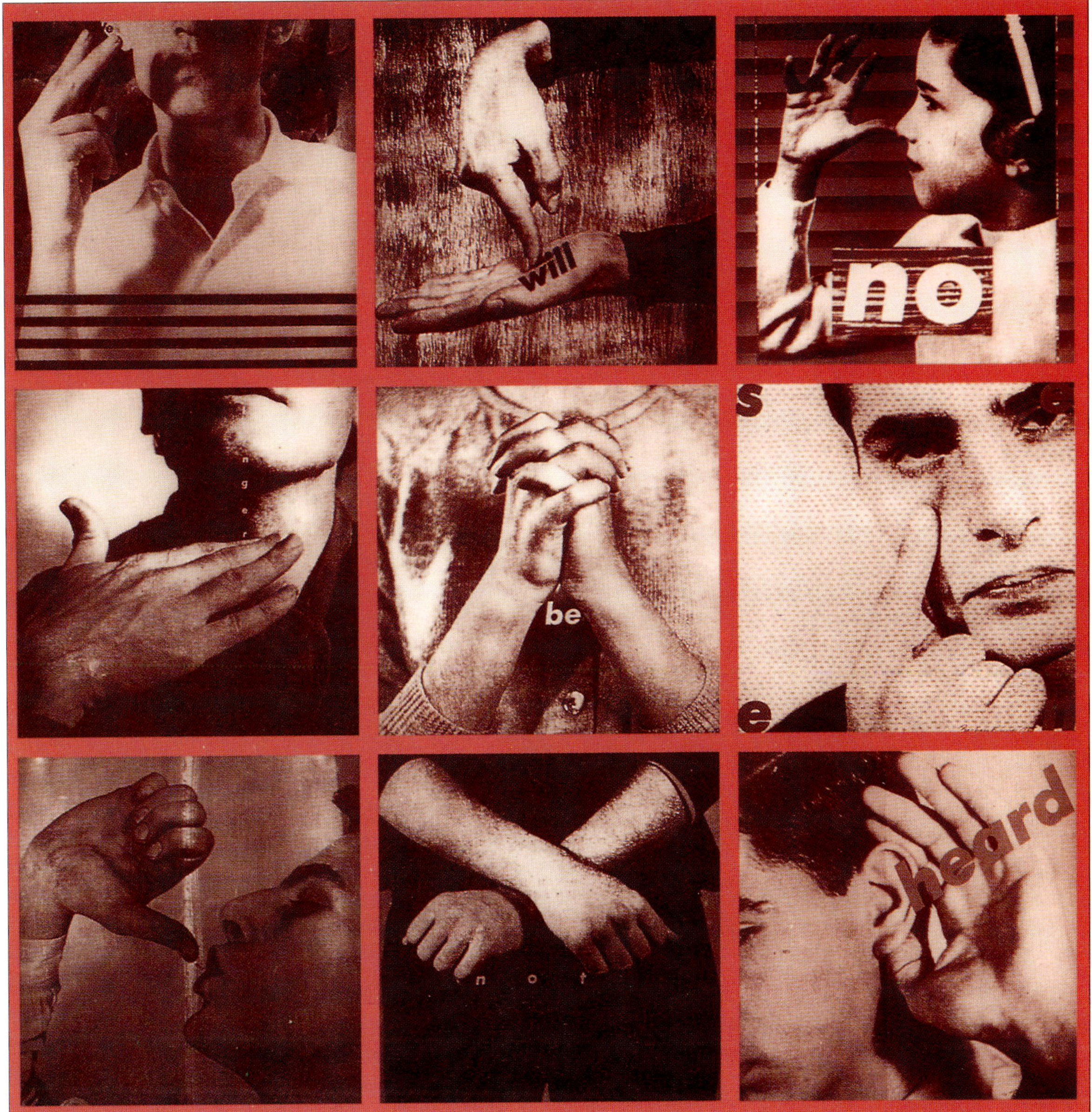

Untitled, (We will no longer be seen and not heard), 1985, photo-lithographs, 9 sheets, each sheet 52 x 52 cm

– *How important is feminist art in New York at the moment? I'm thinking in particular of artists such as Barbara Kruger, Sherrie Levine, Jenny Holzer and Cindy Sherman. Do they think of themselves primarily as 'feminist artists'?*

I can't speak for the individual artists, but what I can say, and I really think it's a kind of triumphant thing, is that there is now an amazing number of very prominent women artists who demand completely as much attention as men and their programme in art has, I would say, absolutely nothing to do with feminism. There was a period when art had to be programmatic to make its point – I'm thinking of the overtly feminist works of Judy Chicago – but now we talk about Barbara Kruger, Jenny Holzer, Jennifer Bartlett, Cindy Sherman, Elizabeth Murray, the list goes on and on, in terms that have absolutely nothing to do with their gender. And the fact that we just think about them as artists *per se* seems to be an enormous triumph. They're very well represented in the galleries and they are, it seems to me, completely integrated into the contemporary art world; their numbers are very very satisfying. In fact there was a recent exhibition in New York, now circulating the United States, called *Making their Mark*, which is really in effect about this theme, namely the feminist movements in art during the last 20 years, and the exhibition itself is really an anthology of terrific artists who happen to be women. And the fact that they are terrific artists and that secondarily they happen to be women seems to indicate that something very good has happened.

– *Finally, are there any young artists in New York whose work interests you and whose names may as yet be unfamiliar to the London art world?*

Nobody I can think of, and I'm not being cagey. I think that the degree of immediate communication around the world is such today, that any young artists I might have heard of, I'm sure would be known in London within minutes. So the chances for artists remaining unfamiliar to the international art world are very slight because communication in the 80s is so instant.

CINDY SHERMAN

'What can be said about the visual arts in a patriarchal order that privileges vision over the other senses? Can we not expect them to be a domain of masculine privilege – as their histories indeed prove them to be – a means, perhaps, of mastering through representation the "threat" posed by the female? In recent years there has emerged a visual arts practice informed by feminist theory and addressed, more or less explicitly, to the issue of representation and sexuality . . . women have begun the long-overdue process of deconstructing femininity. Few have produced new, "positive" images of a revised femininity; to do so would simply supply and thereby prolong the life of the existing representational apparatus . . . Most of these artists . . . work with the existing repertory of cultural imagery – not because they either lack originality or criticise it –but because their subject, feminine sexuality, is always constituted in and as representation, a representation of difference. It must be emphasised that these artists are not primarily interested in what representations say about women; rather, they investigate what representation does to women (for example, the way it invariably positions them as objects of the male gaze) . . .

' Sherman's photographs . . . function as mirror-masks that reflect back at the viewer his own desire (and the spectator posited by this work is invariably male) – specifically, the masculine desire to fix the woman in a stable and stabilising identity. But this is precisely what Sherman's work denies: for while her photographs are always self-portraits, in them the artist never appears to be the same, indeed, not even the same model; while we can presume to recognise the same person, we are forced at the same time to recognise a trembling around the edges of that identity. In a subsequent series of works, Sherman abandoned the film-still format for that of the magazine centrefold, opening herself to charges that she was an accomplice in her own objectification, reinforcing the image of the woman bound by the frame. This may be true; but while Sherman may pose as a pin-up, she still cannot be pinned down.' **Craig Owens**

'It is the power of technologically produced pictures over the human mind and human behaviour which is at the centre of Cindy Sherman's photo-pieces. These works are an excellent reflection of the omnipresent world of the commercial media. She is a photographer, actress, film director, scriptwriter, stylist, make-up assistant, hairdresser, stage designer . . . And although her artistic tool has always been photography, the rhetoric of her art is clearly that of film. One might say that Cindy Sherman projects a whole film into a single photo-piece, a film with only one actress – herself . . . the actress assumes different parts – roles that are actively promoted by films and magazines, and above all by society, which imposes certain behavioural patterns on people, and specially on women . . . Gone is the playfulness of black-and-white photos and also the charmingly nostalgic aura of her "film quotes". It is the element of criticism which has now come to the fore . . . There is a subliminal aggressiveness which emanates from these pictures, a certain rebellion against stereotyped ideals of beauty. "I want that choked-up feeling in your throat," says Cindy Sherman, "which maybe comes from despair or teary-eyed sentimentality: conveying intangible emotions." ' **Klaus Honnef**

Untitled No 96, 1981, colour photograph, 70 x 122 cm

Above: *Untitled No 66*, 1980, colour photograph, 50.8 x 61 cm; *Below*: *Untitled No 74*, 1980, colour photograph, 50.8 x 61 cm

THE WHITNEY BIENNIAL
Coming Up Empty
Kim Levin

Francesc Torres, *Belchite-South Bronx: A Trans-Cultural Landscape*, 1988, video installation

The Whitney Biennial, eagerly awaited by artists, critics and dealers, has become the subject of controversy. Seen by some as a valuable guide to current trends, in touch with the pulse of contemporary New York, it is accused by others of betraying a lack of vision, direction and critical judgement. Kim Levin, of *Village Voice*, here highlights the problems of the 1989 Biennial, which she sees as consolidating rather than challenging the market.

Francesc Torres' installation in the lobby makes the only direct social statement in the 65th version of the show we biennially love to hate. Titled *Oikonomos*, it has tarry black walls, floor-board lights, and a black bronze cast of a Classical Zeus, who wields not his lost thunderbolt but an aluminium baseball bat. Flung in the corner, a racing-car driver's hastily removed, corporate-sponsored clothes. On the big video screen that Zeus confronts, the disenfranchised (another 'race' – black) engage in a growing American enterprise: washing windshields of cars stopped at red lights. A tiny TV that's got the god by his balls offers images of the empowered: stock market traders and congressmen – business as usual. *Oikonomos*, by the way, means 'economics'.

Well, it's not quite the only social statement. There's also the curators' collective introduction to the catalogue, which reads like a product of artificial intelligence, lacking only Philippe de Montebello's canned voice:

> Today's art world is troubled, yet resilient, something like the society it reflects. We have moved into a situation where wealth is the only agreed upon arbiter of value. Capitalism has overtaken contemporary art, quantifying and reducing it to the status of a commodity.

Yup. Speaking of quantifying, with 75 photographs of envelope patterns, 105 broken windowpanes, 172 glass jars filled with paint, a flotilla of 625 small submarines, a vast sea of 10,000 'individual' objects, and an unobtrusive disk in the wall rotating at 3500 rpm (and these are some of the most effective works), this Whitney Museum of American Art Biennial Exhibition is either going for the *Guinness Book of World Records* or proclaiming a state of galloping consumption. The most indirect social statement: *Security of Julia I*, a nearly invisible video-surveillance piece (with mock museum guard) that turns spectators insidiously into printout and spectacle. As for statistics, it took three curators (Richard Armstrong, Richard Marshall, and Lisa Phillips) to write a 35-sentence introduction – that's not quite one sentence per artist in the show.

Q (overheard outside the Whitney): Who's in the Biennial?

A: Who are Lisa Phillips' friends?

We've all grown cynical. In 1985 I said the show was a 'compendium of the safe, the predictable, and the already seen', suffering from 'failure of nerve, ambition and vision'. In 1987 I called it a 'sedate, sober, and generally unassailable presentation of safe art'. This year I'd skip it entirely if Soho weren't suffering from end-of-the-month (end-of-the-decade, end-of-the-century) blahs. This Biennial is handsomer, safer, less ambitious – and more vapid – than ever. It's got some good artists. And some rooms that, as far as installation goes, are striking. Yet the work ends up looking like, or being turned into, decor. This may be the most suave, contentless, conceptless show yet. It's so vacant it's scary. There's really nothing left to say.

Viewer 1: I think people misunderstand the purpose of the Biennial.

Viewer 2: What's the purpose?

Viewer 1: I think there isn't any purpose.

This country's only regular museum roundup, so to speak, no

longer even proposes to discover new work. Having gone through a number of changes of agenda since the days when it was an uneven extravaganza of work we'd never seen in New York before, the Whitney's goal in the 80s hasn't been to seek out artists around the country, but to provide a top-40 survey 'of the most important and challenging work produced in America over the past two years'. What is left unsaid, of course, is that in doing so the museum relinquishes to the market any front-line curatorial function: this is work that's already been collected and shown. As a quick course in remedial gallery going, the Biennial's also, speaking of economics, a pernicious closed system that validates and consolidates the art market. 'Slam the hell out of it,' whispered a museum guard. 'That's not what's happening around the country. It's out there but they're too lazy to look for it.'

In putting a show of this sort together there are pitfalls on all sides. One question, which no one is asking, is whether a national Biennial is an obsolete idea now that the nomadic art world has spread across the globe – or, to be more precise, now that we in New York have begun to discover what's been going on elsewhere. But for a decade the Biennial, like the nation, has been suffering from other problems: diminished expectations, inertia, conservatism, lack of vision, lack of direction. Any competent curator could assemble a show like this with eyes half-closed in a matter of weeks.

New York's spaces for contemporary art, in comparison with those in Europe and Asia, are cramped. But why does the show become more exclusionary each year (5 artists, not counting film and video, in '85, 44 in '87, 40 now)? And why can't the Whitney use its sacrosanct third floor or satellite spaces? Why can't the 284-page catalogue contain something more than 'descriptions of the works and biographical information on each artist' plus the quick intro? Something thoughtful and cohesive, for example, on the state of art over the past two years, or the relative position of American art in the world? Some attempt to explain why, over the course of the 80s, the predominant sensibility-of-choice – reflected in Biennial selections – has moved from frenzied apocalypse to the synthetic, the sterile, and the comatose? I'd even welcome a zeitgeist tale, any sign of resistance to crass economics. 'Make a list of all the forgotten artists from past Biennials. Trace the show's history. Be prepared to find out that no one at the Whitney remembers', suggested a friend.

Maybe the film, video, and performance works will counter the lack of social, political, and personal content on floors and walls, but as I've said before, involved video doesn't make up for devalued art. Saying the show has parts that look good isn't the same as saying *it's* good. An exhibition is, in a sense, the curators' work of conceptual art.

Reader's Digest is involved in funding this show. Its Biennial is the gallery excerpt, the fit-for-family, abridged selection-of-the-month. And because any group of art objects that shares a place and time is socially and politically relevant, intentionally or not, the Whitney Biennial is a microcosm of 1989 America: a reflection of leveraged buyouts, insider trades, junk bonds, major deficits, and enormous dependence on credit. We don't know exactly whether it's the art, the museum, or something larger that's bankrupt. Everybody's passing the buck.

Allan McCollum, *Individual Works*, 1987-8, installation

The fundamental desire to discover and understand the governing logic of thought and action no doubt lies behind the continuing appeal of conceptual approaches to art-making. More recently, such approaches have also seemed an appropriate means to analyse the accelerated visual data that comprises daily existence, almost to the exclusion of all other sensate reception. Conceptual work profits from its own camouflage as data, however aestheticised. Nevertheless, the need for direct, unmediated experience is still desperately felt. Many artists have sought through the force of the primitive and the explicitly handmade to strengthen a physical and emotional encounter.

The notion that this exhibition is perilously obsessed with novelty is as inaccurate as it is parochial. Large survey exhibitions such as this gain strength from the inclusion of younger, untried artists. About two-thirds of the artists in this Biennial have not previously shown at the Whitney Museum. They are represented here with several examples of works in a context that also includes the ongoing achievements of other, better-known artists who collectively form the infrastructure that supports and sustains their younger colleagues. Incorporating the new helps clarify continuities and changes among generations of creative people. The need is for more exhibitions of an exploratory nature, rather than those that claim definitiveness and authority – always temporary qualities at best.

Artists are struggling to develop a visual language which can cope with the demands of the present, while seeking values that will endure. Contemporary art, as accomplished and eerie as the civilisation we have constructed, continues to sustain us with its vital, regenerative power.

from the organisers' introduction

Francesc Torres, *Belchite-South Bronx: A Trans-Cultural Landscape*, 1988, videotape. 'Torres' installations and videotapes explore the roots of human aggression by examining specific historical events and social and political processes . . . In *Belchite-South Bronx*, Torres uses archival footage of the destruction of Belchite as well as videotape he shot there and in the South Bronx to juxtapose the histories and cultures of these two communities. Belchite is destroyed in a war against oppression; in the South Bronx, footage of youths playing basketball offers a metaphor for combat and suggests the strength of their resolve to exist within and perhaps prevail over capitalism . . .'

Nam June Paik, *Living with The Living Theater*, 1989, video still. 'His wide-ranging interest in all forms of art making has shaped his aesthetic, bringing multiple resourses and concepts to his individual performances, compositions, videotape projects . . . In his hands, video becomes a vehicle of expression that alters the conventional perception of media technologies and reveals their potential to stimulate and challenge . . . Paik's art is about memory . . . Using a dazzling array of video-processing techniques, Paik becomes a magical trickster who plays with the images to vividly recreate the anarchic life and idealism of The Living Theater. As Paik perceives it, The Living Theater remains a vital exemplar of the hope for social change that art can express.'

Chris Burden, *All the Submarines of the United States of America*, 1987, installation. 'In the late 1960s and 1970s, Chris Burden first addressed his radical inquisition into ethical responsibility in a series of actions on himself . . . As his notoriety grew, he turned his ferocity toward broader aspects of society . . . In *All the Submarines of the United States of America* 625 cardboard, wood, and wire submarines, each about 8 inches long, are hung from the ceiling like a miniature flotilla. Their printed names occupy a nearby wall . . . Burden's method of seeking unquestionable truth in the irrational is almost overcome by the atypical lyricism of this piece. But in focusing on deeds and their consequences, he manages to menace and disrupt the status quo.'

Allan McCollum, *Individual Works*, 1987-88, installation. 'Each unique "individual work" is in fact made from some combination of 150 different elements originally cast from domestic objects: cat toys, candy molds, drawer pulls, and bottle caps . . . In fact *Individual Works* can be read as a parody of the store, where the excess of goods on parade reaches such a critical mass that it has a paralytic effect on one's ability to make choices . . . A commentary on the artwork as commodity, as alienated goods, McCollum's individual works are abundant, available, and nonexclusive tokens of authenticity. The aura of the handmade object has been supplanted by the aura of mass production.'

Meg Webster, *Salt Cone*, 1988, installation at the XLIII Biennale di Venezia. 'The merging of the organic and geometric, of landscape and architecture, remains an ongoing concern for Webster. Whether earth, wood, mud, hay, salt, flour, sand, or water . . . there is a strong elemental presence, a smell, a texture, and a light-reflecting and absorbing quality that emanates from the unmediated material. Webster generally works the materials by hand into softened geometries that bear the imprint of her methods . . . Temporality – proof that things are mutable – is an important aspect of Webster's art . . . Though she indirectly evokes environmental concerns, her main achievement is an insistence on the primal experience of direct perception.'

KON-SU NAM

Jeffrey Wechsler

The Doll, 1986, oil, 50.8 x 61cm

A visitor approaching the studio of Kon-Su Nam in recent months was likely to receive a first impression of the artist's work not visually, but aurally. Through the wall of the studio could be heard a succession of similar sounds, rhythmic and repetitive, hard to identify, perhaps the dull thumps of two hard objects making strong contact. Upon entering the studio one might momentarily forget the sound, for covering the walls are large expanses of raw canvas covered with row upon row of black numerals, each canvas containing thousands upon thousands of individual numerals. The canvases vary in size, but are of large dimensions: some are 105 x 92 inches, some 92 x 240 inches. And surrounded by this sea of numbers, one would find the artist and the source of the sound. She is manually stamping, one by one, individual numerals onto canvas from one-by-two-inch printer's blocks. Each block is inked, positioned one-quarter inch from the last, and a numeral is transferred onto canvas by a blow of a hammer. The repeating sound was the meeting of block and hammer, and the numerals arrayed around the walls are the result of untold hours of single-minded effort.

But to what end is this labour? The effect of Nam's art is equally as remarkable as the labour required to create it. The number pieces represent one aspect, albeit the most obsessive one, of recent serial works by Nam which have crystallised in the past year or so the artist's themes and intentions. Nam has stated that the masses of numerals symbolise an infinite expanse of humanity, individual yet anonymous, and more specifically that innumerable quantity of individuals who have suffered at the hands of others, who have suffered anonymous fates meted out by anonymous bureaucracies or dehumanised individuals. To understand Nam's intentions, it is well to record her own thoughts. The artist has noted:

> I believe the true mission of my art to be the expulsion of all things that cause divisions within and between human beings leading to violence, disaster, and hatred . . . to achieve its ends, it would have to force the audience to confront itself. To do this, it activates the audience by operating directly on the sensory apparatus in a way that bypasses the conscious mind . . . I want my work to appeal to the conscience of the audience, thereby placing the spectators on moral, spiritual, and ethical trial.

The vast fields of numerals certainly can assault the audience by overwhelming scale, and can 'by-pass the conscious mind by presenting numbers in too great a quantity to grasp in terms of everyday comprehension, whether mathematical or psychological. Yet in her art, Nam also seeks to confront herself. She strongly believes that all great art is 'self-reflexive'; it must truly divulge the character of its creator intellectually and spiritually. Therefore, Nam's approach to art involves a complex interaction of carefully considered materials, techniques, and imagery chosen to express various levels of meaning and experience. The number pieces are part of a group of serial works that deal with the concept of victimisation and power (with implications of the Holocaust). These concepts are used as 'universal issues' with diverse and generalised ramifications beyond the specific time and place of the European tragedy, referring to 'past, present and future loss'. To illustrate these points, one may consider a recent installation by the artist that incorporated a number piece. One section of the installation consisted of nine faces, each forcefully rendered in shades of black, white, and grey, each face nearly filling a separate unstretched square of canvas surrounded by a deep black frame, and overlaid by a square of black screening. These unsettling, unidentified faces are 'dehumanised' and seen as part of a 'compartmentalised' social system by means of the rigidly ordered arrangement that contains them. At first glance, this multiple array of bleak faces might appear threatening to the viewer. Indeed, the artist is concerned with 'the impersonal force that comes from the many', both in action and 'subconscious effect'. However, in the title of the piece, stressed through capitalisation, is the word 'RESISTANCE'. The role of the individuals can therefore be deduced as a positive one, and in fact the visual strength of the nine-part grid symbolises for the artist a projection of a combined force against evil. In place of specific identifications, which could otherwise confirm or deny the viewer's initial impression of the faces, the verbal 'clue' in the title provides a means to determine if the individuals embody evil or fight against it. In either case, their personal ideals and actions could cause them to become separated from the society in which they find themselves. Obscured behind screening and set apart by the black squares, their division from the general populace has left them 'caged' in state- and self-imposed isolation.

The other section of the installation confronts the viewer with one of the canvases filled with numerals, hanging from a metal bar, which is itself supported by large metal hooks. The materials and their arrangement carry further social and psychological implications. The use of numerals as representatives of victimised humanity underscores the depersonalisation and 'loss of individuality' found in many aspects of modern society. As mentioned above, the purpose of the expanse of numerals is to 'numb the senses' of the viewer, to overwhelm an attempt at easy comprehension of the situations it symbolises; equating humanity with a sea of numbers, the quantification of loss is, in effect, incalculable. Additionally, the abstract nature of 'numbers and mathematics' evokes a 'cold and dry' quality from many observers, an effect that the artist finds applicable to the 'cold and dry feeling one gets from cruel, evil people' or 'acts of brutality'. The thick metal bar above the numerals also alludes to that cold, dry quality in its 'rigid, technological' appearance.

The enormous amount of time and labour devoted to making every field of numerals is of particular significance to the artist. It is an arduous task to individually ink, position and hand-stamp thousands of randomly chosen numerals onto the canvases spread on her studio floor. Yet by doing so, Nam endures a 'physical sacrifice', a repetitive, down-on-the-hands-and-knees procedure 'demanding considerable time and discomfort' that in its own way becomes an obeisance to the larger issue that inspired her actions, a sacred, meditative, healing procedure. The 'concept of repetition' is important, for it symbolises the 'anonymity' of the victims, and the 'mindless, mechanical' method of their victimisation. Even the act of printing the numeral-block, stamping it with a hammer blow, can be seen as symbolic of the repeated acts of violence against individuals: individuals anonymously identified only as numbers.

With the incorporation of unusual materials and objects such as metal bars, screening and rope, Nam's recent work shows an impressive evolution beyond the relatively traditional paintings she made only a few years ago. A striking feature about the recent works, from about the past year, is how they integrate in a coherent way a wide range of simultaneous visual and philosophical changes in Nam's art. Parallel evolutions and amplifications of formal theory, content, media and imagery have been intertwined into a tautly drawn and controlled fibre of process and metaphor. In the number pieces, the installation described above, and works such as *The Twenty-fifth Hour,* Nam's art has reached new levels of clarity, power and subtlety. The evolution of several aspects of the work can be stated briefly through examples of earlier paintings from 1986 to 1987.

The 'universal' human figure, represented symbolically, is a dominating presence in these works, painted in a robustly three-dimensional manner with forceful modelling and highlighting of forms. When in groups, the figures convey a sense of isolation. In a few works, masks are depicted with human expressions; actual faces have a mask-like quality. All these devices suggest hypocrisy, misrepresentation, and injustice. Ominous, oppressive psychological states are evoked, with metaphysical undertones. The figures are placed in environments of isolation or apparent powerlessness: a woman lies tensely on a table in a room empty except for a curtain and a bare light bulb hanging above her face; a man struggles against a chain binding him to what appears to be a chalice set on a window ledge. Around 1987, Nam's painting turned toward a much flatter and schematic style. She specifically rejected 'brushiness' and impastoed techniques as visually distracting; these were deemed extraneous painterly elements that got in the way of presenting her ideas in a direct fashion.

Consequently, her work became more involved with the relationship of three-dimensional form to the two-dimensional picture plane. *The Bather* is a work of transitional formal significance to Nam, in which she explores the concepts of Modernism that had been troubling issues for her, such as the integrity and literalness of the canvas-support-as-object. Here, a prone figure, itself somewhat flattened by its pale colour and blue halation, reclines within an ultra-violet light tanning machine. This device, threatening in its mechanical sterility, darkness, and essentially unnatural function, is rendered with a staining technique, thus depicting a solid form by means of a diaphanous surface. The artist also places the steel-like structure against areas of raw, unpainted canvas, reducing spatial illusionism.

The use of colour in Nam's art has undergone a dramatic change. Earlier work tended to avail itself of a full chromatic range, often with glowing hues, such as deep, saturated reds that symbolised evil, violence, and intensity of feeling. As her focus on deriving her art from direct intellectual and spiritual sources intensified, a shift toward metallic colour occurred, reflecting and enhancing that spirituality. Bright multi-coloured compositions were gradually withdrawn from her art. 'When I see human tragedy, I don't see colours,' says the artist, 'Black and white are what I feel.' Colours became a distraction, an unwanted source of visual delectation, a quality increasingly irrelevant to her purposes.

Perhaps Nam's most radical stylistic development is her use of words and numbers as primary imagery for much of her art. For an artist who places ideas at the core of her work, the visually communicative medium for ideas – words – were logically the direct way to convey meaning. Nam began to use those texts which she found particularly appropriate to express profound experiences. Her first work consisting entirely of words was derived from Goethe's *The Sorrows of Young Werther.* The notions of quotation and paraphrasing are viewed by Nam as empathetic processes that transcend simple transference of a text. A selected writer is recognised as a kindred spirit whose ideas and feelings coincide with those of the artist. Poems and other writings therefore become another form of artistic medium – like any other symbol, image, or material – for conveying the artist's own thoughts or ideas. So involved is Nam now with the conceptual and intellectual underpinnings of her art that she no longer creates traditional sketches or drawings to plan her work. Instead she keeps notes of thoughts and feelings, at times based on remembered writings, at times drawn from within herself. This fundamentally ideational methodology conforms with Nam's desire to reach to the 'essence' of her themes. It also allows her to create more spontaneously, in the sense that an idea can mature along varied routes, encouraging exploration of new materials or formats. For example, to investigate a fresh means

Above: *Soliloquy*, 1988, acrylic, 137.2 x 177.8 x 9.5 cm; *Below*: *100446,100447 . . . RESISTANCE*, 1988-9, acrylic and screen, each panel 73.7 x 73.7 x 9.2cm

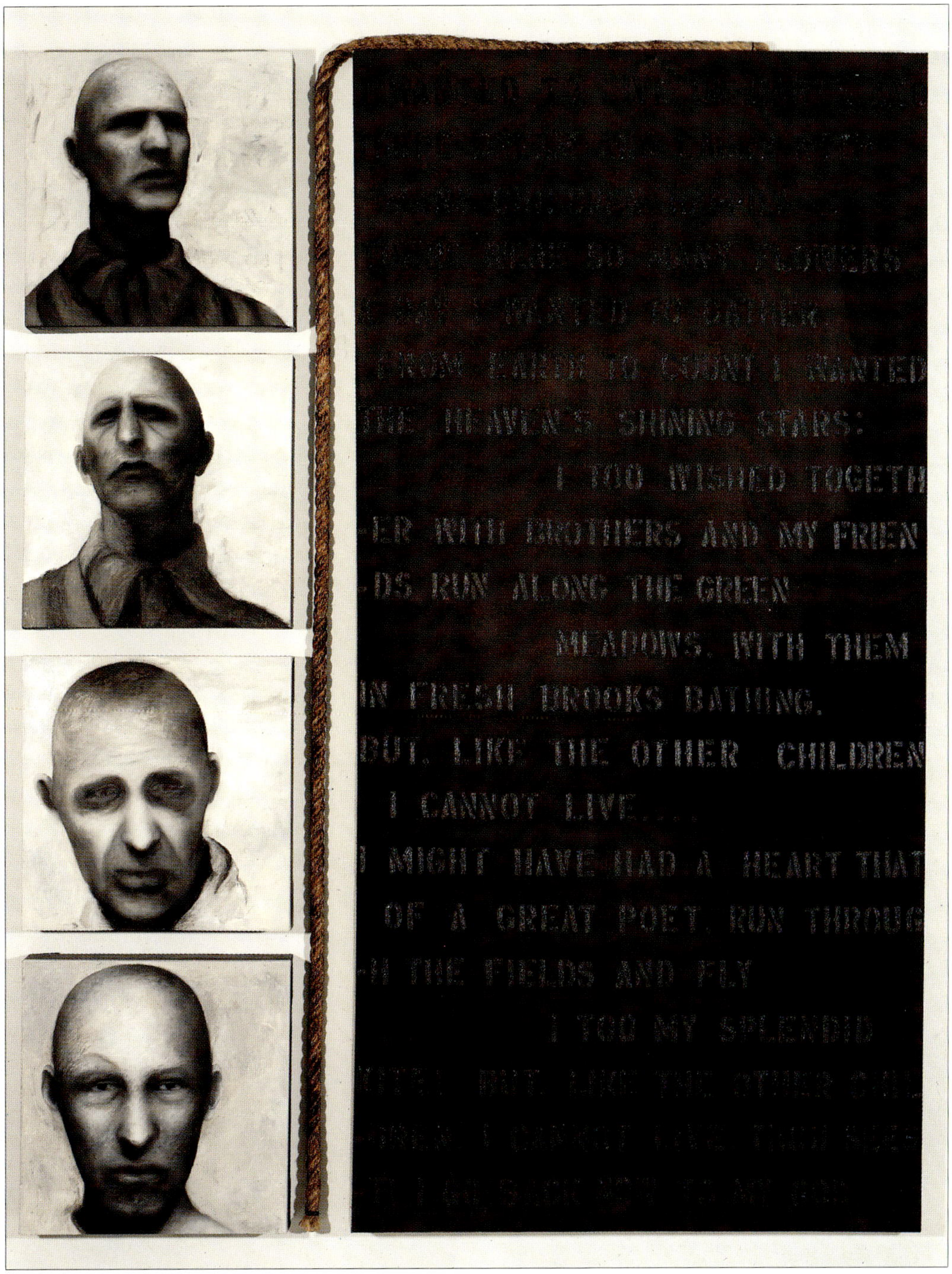

Above: *The Twenty-Fifth Hour*, 1988, mixed media, four panels; *Below L and R: 100446, 100447... RESISTANCE*, details

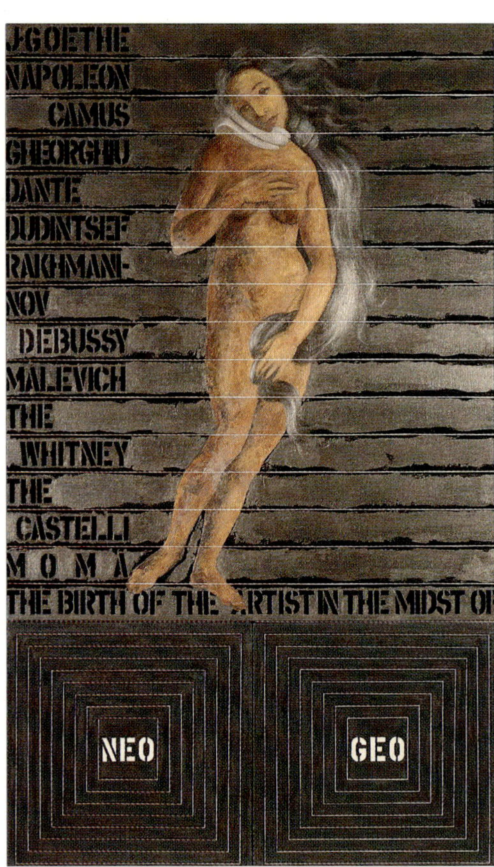

L to R: The Artist Contemplating, 1987, oil/acrylic diptych; *The Birth of the Artist in the Midst of NEO-GEO*, 1988, acrylic triptych

of showing the importance of repetitious activity in the making of the number pieces, Nam has recently used video, a medium she had no previous experience with, to create a work of art dealing with that process. Her physical activity, however, was modified for the video to reinforce a subtle meaning behind the act of stamping. Nam used a particularly candenced speed of hammering to elicit the meditative quality of the act; she relates the movements to the studied, rhythmic striking of bells or gongs performed by participants in Buddhist devotional ceremonies.

In the work entitled *The Twenty-fifth Hour*, the viewer can see encapsulated the converging stylistic developments of formal properties, imagery, and careful deployment of words and materials. At the left of this work are four images, black and white renderings of faces, close up, with some showing enough of the shoulders to reveal a striped costume. Many observers might identify these individuals as prisoners of concentration camps, victims of the Holocaust. The faces are painted on deep stretchers, the image-as-object concept unexpectedly reminding viewers of the pure painting concerns of the artist, even within this forlorn theme. The painted surfaces of the faces extend around onto the edges of the stretchers for a few fractions of an inch; the face is stressed as a symbol of humanity within a larger context, artistic and philosophical. Many visual relationships have been incorporated into the structure and imagery of this work: the solidity of the faces on the four squares contrasts with the amorphous, receding spatial effect of the rectangular panel on the right; the faces are dark, black, organic shapes situated on flat, white, geometric picture planes; the recessive effect of the background of the right panel plays against the reflectivity of the letters set upon it.

On the right panel is a poem, expressing the artist's state of mind, in letters first stencilled in outline and then filled in with paint. The lettered text itself raises other issues for the artist: Nam's fascination with technology (typewriting and stencilling are mechanical means for creating words) and her ceaseless investigation of Modernist pictorial principles. The unusual surface quality of the panel draws the viewers in, their curiosity impelling them toward deeper personal reflections upon what they read. The words glitter on the black-brown background, hazy irregular areas evoking stains or burns ('indelible marks of a wound' suggests the artist). It is the meaning and tone of the verse, its relation to the context of the piece which is important.

> I wanted to live on earth and there dream and laugh with many children happily. There were so many flowers a day I wanted to gather, from earth to count I wanted the heaven's shining stars: I too wished together with my brothers and my friends run along the green meadows with them in fresh brooks bathing. But like the other children I cannot live . . .

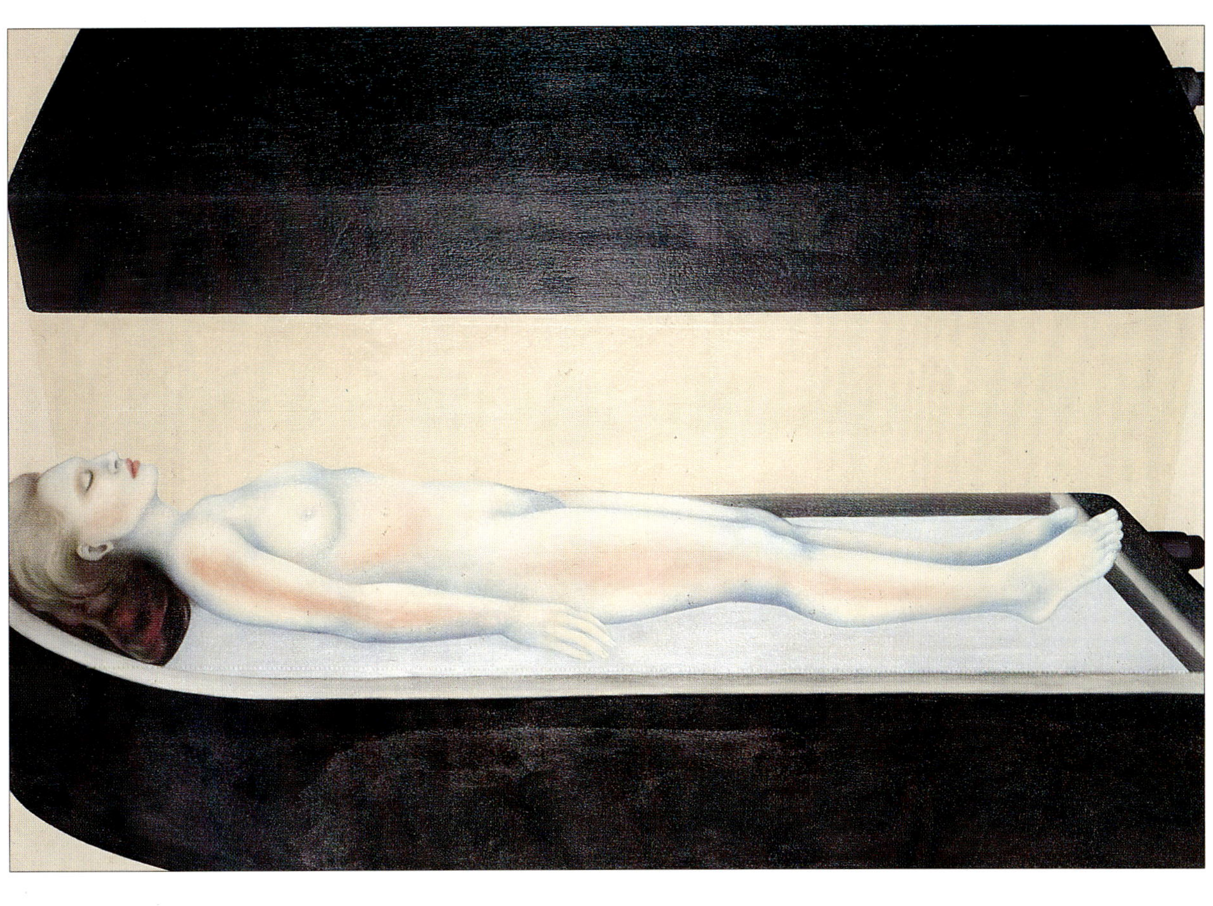

The Bather, 1989, oil/acrylic on raw canvas, 114.3 x 167.6 x 7.6cm

> I might have had a heart that of a great poet, run through the fields and fly I too my splendid kite! But, like the other children, I cannot live. Thou zest! I go back now to my God.

In the context of the faces, the restriction to black and white, the stark and solid geometry of the canvases, the dissolving and evanescent nature of the lettering – in all these relationships, the poem carries an ineffable poignancy, an abyssal and timeless perception of the human condition. And between the poem panel and the four faces, the viewer sees a rope. It lies on top of the poem panel and, after being supported by those fragile, plaintive words, drops over the side to hang limply next to the faces. Again, almost shockingly in this setting, the rope is meticulously positioned to carry a formal, visual function within the overall composition of the work, unifying the sections with a linear motif and an offset spatial level. Yet the rope implies a weakened physical presence, hanging by the anonymous victims, unable to support itself, lacking power. And the rope is burnt.

Kon-Su Nam's work seems to have reached a high plateau of urgency for the artist. One might think that one or two of the number pieces would suffice to convey the need for identification with the nameless victims. But about five large canvases swarming with numerals have been made, and more are planned. The suffering goes on and the number pieces, for some indeterminate time, will also go on. Victimisation exists, continual and reciprocal: how can one, the artist questions, determine 'an end'? So as Kon-Su Nam elaborates new ideas on her 'universal themes', they are accepted as projects that 'must be done', in whatever medium or method is appropriate.

From outside the studio of Kon-Su Nam, the hammer blows can be heard, one by one, rhythmically, like a meditative singsong of penance. On the surface of *Soliloquy,* her initial word piece based on writings by Goethe, appear the words: 'When I see . . . how any comfort we may derive from certain points of inquiry is merely a dreamlike kind of resignation, in which we paint our prison walls with coloured figures and luminous prospects – all this . . . leaves me speechless'. In the studio, the numerals are randomly chosen, assigned the next position in the precisely ordered rows, and struck, decisively, leaving an imprint – with some individual meaning – soon to be lost amid thousands more. On the surface of *Soliloquy* the text continues: 'I withdraw into my inner self and there discover a world – it is true, rather of vague perceptions and dim desires than of creative power and vital force. And then everything swims before my senses, and I go on smiling at the outer world like someone in a dream.'

Jasper Johns, *Untitled*, 1988, encaustic, 96.5 x 66cm

LEO CASTELLI

An *Art & Design* Interview

Robert Rauschenberg, *Trilogy from the Bellini Series*, 1987, 3 unigraphs, 153.7 x 97.8cm

Widely regarded as the most influential dealer in New York, Leo Castelli has played a crucial role in the development of art since the early 60s. In this interview, he discusses his aims as a dealer, the criteria which have determined his choice of artists such as Jasper Johns, Robert Rauschenberg, David Salle and the Starn Twins, his relationship with artists and critics, and his views on the curent trends and attitudes of the New York art market.

– *Do you see New York as the centre, the focal point of the international contemporary art market?*

Well, I think that this is taken for granted now by just about everybody, except some people who for many different reasons may think that Cologne, or Paris, or London are the real centres, which would be wide of the mark of course.

– *As a dealer, how do you respond to criticisms of the art world in New York: the accusations of hype, the criticisms of art as a commodity, and of artists as businessmen, simply responding to the demands of a consumer market?*

Well I'll tell you something. There are galleries and galleries. My gallery's work is to show my artists, the artists who belong to my stable, artists whom I have had for more than 30 years, and I do it in the traditional way. I just give them the best shows I can. I do, without exaggerating, a good announcement or a catalogue if necessary, and I hope for the best. I continue to do this in the same old way, although prices do of course go up in what you call the secondary market. Tremendous sums are paid at auctions for painters such as Jasper Johns or Lichtenstein, but I'm not responsible for that. When it comes to my shows – I had for instance a show of Jasper Johns, which is rare because he produces very little, and one of Lichtenstein which will occur sometime in the fall – I will not, after finding that prices of two million, three million dollars are being paid for his early work, increase my prices accordingly. They just increase in the normal way as they always do, by 10 or 20 percent, in spite of the fact that there is a tremendous demand for the work of all these important artists. One could, of course, speculate and not sell them at the moment with their shows, but that would be entirely unethical and I wouldn't do that kind of thing. Other people may do, I don't know.

– *Donald Judd has criticised the art world of the 80s, writing that 'The public and also young artists, not being able to know better, begin to think that the art business somehow has something to do with art. Commerce is not art.' Are artists on the whole critical of the commercial market in New York?*

I don't know what artists think of other dealers. I'm involved with my artists and they've never been critical of what I'm doing. I think that the good artists – some names I have already mentioned – just pursue their work and that's what there're involved with, not in making money. I actually feel the same way: I'm not here to make money, I'm here to do a good job for my artists, and have an ambition for them to be recognised all over the world. I've done that all my life, and will continue doing the same thing. Money is not at all my aim, although it is of course necessary to do a good job. I need plenty of employees and a large organisation because my painters are travelling all over the world, to various shows, museums, other dealers and so on, so they need money too. But that's not the aim of the gallery, to make money.

– *How influential are dealers in controlling and determining trends in the market?*

Dealers are really less important now than auction houses. Auction houses certainly are much more influential in determining the prices of the more famous artists than the dealers. Alternatively, not galleries like mine, but those that deal espe-

Frank Stella, *The Crotch*, 1988, mixed media on cast aluminium, 520.7 x 250.2 x 137.2cm

cially in the secondary market are very influential, sure; galleries that deal with very expensive and very desirable paintings and can ask any price for them, and because they are rare any price will go. So it is the auction houses principally and then some important dealers in the secondary market who determine the prices; we just follow suit. We follow suit in the sense that if very high prices are obtained for paintings of one or another of my painters, I do not increase the prices of artists I have in my gallery right away; I mean they will increase by slow degrees. I won't jump suddenly and say, well, if something was 100,000 dollars today, and then I see that a painting by the same artist is being sold for 200,000 dollars, I won't say that the next paintings that I have will be 200,000 dollars. But of course we will also be interested in auction prices and secondary market prices. There has been a quantum leap in the past two years, and the auction prices obtained at Christies and Sotheby's certainly triggered this tremendous increase in prices.

– *To what extent do dealers control the development of artists whom they represent, not only in terms of market prices but in terms of stylistic development?*

The stylistic development, of course the dealers are responsible for that. It's not the auction houses or the secondary market dealers who do that; that's our job. We find new artists and then, if we've chosen well, we make them into important artists. That happened in the 60s and happens still now, with young artists, like Koons or Halley or Vaisman, or the Starn Twins. We find those artists and we promote them; it's not the auction houses that do that.

– *How do you find new artists and what criteria determine your choice?*

Well, sometimes you find them in the group shows. For example, Jasper Johns, whom nobody knew back in 1957, appeared for the first time, very young, at a show in the Jewish Museum, and that's where I saw one of his paintings for the first time. That was one way. Then Lichtenstein, for instance, a few years later, back in 1961, came to the gallery with a number of paintings which he brought on the top of his station waggon, and showed them to me. I asked him, well, why was he coming to see me, and his answer was, 'I can't think of any other gallery that would even look at my paintings'. So he came to me and indeed I found them very interesting and then took him on. Then in the case of Stella, for instance, another important painter who I've handled over the

Frank Stella, *Stubbs' Supper*, 1988, mixed media on fabricated aluminium, 219.1 x 308 x 123.5cm

years, a critic friend of mine said that he'd seen some amazing paintings the day before at the studio of a young man called Frank Stella, and why didn't I go and see them? So I did go, and there you are. Or certain artists for instance appear in smaller galleries. A year ago, for example, two or three artists appeared in small galleries in East Village and we saw them; they of course didn't want to stay there, so some of them we got that way.

– *Is it important that you, as the dealer, personally like the art you represent?*

It's not only important, it's essential. If I don't like it, I don't take it. Not only do I have to like it, but I have to consider it important. I have to use my brains and find out, is this really important, is this really a new trend or does it belong to a new trend, is it bound to stay, has it something new to say, is it original? I have to ask myself all those questions, and if the questions are not answered, or negatively answered, then I won't ever take an artist on. As a matter of fact, as I have probably proved in my career, over a period of years I have picked about the best painters that appeared in America. That's done, not by accident, but because I'm trying to find them.

– *How did you find your youngest artist David Salle, and what interests you about his work?*

David Salle was at Mary Boone's – she found him. Then Mary Boone felt, at that time, that it would be nice if we could share him. And so that's what we're doing. Salle's work is quite original; to begin with, it's good work, aesthetically speaking. It's interestingly structured, it conveys interesting ideas, and it's good painting. It answers all the questions I have about an artist. He's a very strong artist.

– *Robert Rosenblum sees the work of Rosenquist and Rauschenberg, both artists whom you represent, as very much part of the background to Salle's art.*

All that happened a long time ago. Rosenquist I found in the early days of the Pop movement, Rauschenberg even earlier than that. They both were and are very original painters and have stayed that way through the years.

– *A tendency in the paintings of David Salle and in the work of many other contemporary artists is to quote from art history. What do you think of this retrospective mood in contemporary art at the moment?*

Artists will do whatever they want to do and actually, through

Starn Twins, *Blue Lisa*, 1987, toned silver print, 215.9 x 134.6cm

too rapid, they change their life-style too rapidly. But the really good artists are involved with their art more than anything else and that's their focus, all the rest is secondary. And I think they would prefer to go back to simple conditions, rather than that the art world should be influential in what they're doing. But of course I'm thinking of the really good artists.

– What do you think of the work of Barbara Kruger, Cindy Sherman, Sherrie Levine etc? Are women artists well represented in the galleries?

I like Sherrie Levine's work very much; I buy for my own collection works of artists that I like and Levine is one of those. There are certainly some very good women artists that we have around: Levine is certainly one of them, also Cindy Sherman and Barbara Kruger who is a very interesting artist. Women artists are now much more sure of themselves, they do not paint any more with the feeling that they have to struggle because they're women, they are important artists in their own right. I think their attitude has changed a great deal. Jennifer Bartlett, for example, is another artist I would want to mention in this context.

– How interested are you in 'alternative' art – performance, video, environmental etc? Do you think these artists have failed in their attempt to resist the commercial market?

That's something that had its vogue a while ago and perhaps isn't practiced as much now as it used to be, say 10 years or 15 years back. It was a moment when artists wanted to do ever larger works and didn't want to have the taint of commercialism attached to their art and therefore went out into the wilderness to do things there. This was the attitude that provoked this type of art; it has now changed very much and I think most artists today are very pleased and happy to show in galleries.

– What role does critical writing play in determining the success of an artist and in influencing market trends? What is your relationship, as a dealer, with the critics in New York?

Well, critical writing of course – depending on who does it – has its importance. The critics, collectors, museum curators and directors, and of course the galleries, are all influential in creating an image of the artist. All good critics are an important component there. But, as with any gallery or museum, they cannot make or break an artist. There has to be a certain consensus, and critical writing of course is part of that consensus. But we don't work together, there is no influence that we want to exercise on the opinions of the critics; we don't do that here in New York. It's a very honest situation that we have here, unlike perhaps other places where the critics are constantly influenced by galleries in one way or another. No, we are quite impartial, nobody tries to influence them. Sometimes I'm furious at a critic because he writes a bad review about an artist or a show that I consider good, but there is nothing that I can do about it. I won't phone that critic and say to him that he has misbehaved, although sometimes I am really very furious if the artists are not reviewed at all, say, by *The New York Times*, but I won't then phone John Russell and say why has this magnificent show been neglected? No, we don't do that.

–What are the current New York trends and do you see any new tendencies developing, particularly among young artists?

Well, we had this so-called 'Neo-Geo' group of people, which is just a misnoma because few were actually geometrical, and we've mentioned them all except Bickerton perhaps. They reacted against the Neo-Expressionist vogue that we had coming from Italy and Germany, which was quite dominant in the late 70s and the beginning of the 80s, and these young people appeared I think in reaction to that. They are very cool and I think that their inspiration comes in part from Pop Art and then from that eternal, great man who influenced everybody, Marcel Duchamp. So that's the last trend. After that the Starn Twins appeared and their work is unrelated to everything; I think it's very very good; I show them in my gallery, and I think that's the last really important development that I've seen. There is no new trend that I can discern now. But this does not mean we should doubt the future in any way: the pendulum keeps swinging from one way of doing to another and sometimes of course there are multiple trends but there is always, I would say, a dominant trend at any one time. I do feel very optimistic, very hopeful about the future: art is eternal and I think there will always be good art. And as far as the high prices are concerned, they are inevitable – it's the old law of demand and supply.

Robert Mapplethorpe, *Portrait of Leo Castelli*

Jeff Koons, Peter Halley, *New York Art Now*, Saatchi Collection, Sept 1987, installation view

POP ART II – JEFF KOONS & CO

Michael Compton

Jeff Koons, *L to R*: *Saint John the Baptist*, 1988, polychromed porcelain, 143.5 x 76.2 x 62.2 cm; *Naked*, 1988-9, polychromed porcelain, 115.6 x 68.6 x 68.6 cm

While leafing through recent art journals, I noticed more articles on Jeff Koons and Andy Warhol than on any other artists. The simultaneous dominance of two such figures is plainly no coincidence, neither has the resemblance of a certain art of the late 1980s to Pop passed unremarked. One curiosity is that, although this art has been extensively reported, it has not yet acquired any stable name. I shall therefore refer to it as Pop Art II.

The failure of a name to emerge probably has to do with the fact that this art is recognisable by a sort of theory associated with it rather than by a style or look, a theory that relates equally to a form of abstract art, 'Neo Geo'[1] and to 'Neo Pop'[2] – the art of appropriation, transformation or simulation of commercial products. The neatest example of the common ground is Peter Halley, both as writer and painter.[3] To oversimplify, Halley seems to argue that abstraction is the vice of Capitalism; that abstract art is a manifestation of this, as are the control circuits of electronic machines. Therefore, as a means of deconstruction, he has painted simulations of abstract pictures that also resemble circuit diagrams.

In Britain the theory of the information environment, covering both abstract and what were later called appropriationist manifestations, flourished in the late 50s when the metonymy on control system circuitry was also employed as a means of visualisation. Robyn Denny, Dick Smith and Ralph Rumney made a maze-like installation in *Spaces,* 1959, modelling social control. The irony is that the interest in circuitry, which had emerged some years earlier in the group that formed the seed bed of Pop Art (Hamilton, Paolozzi, McHale, Alloway, Banham etc), was based on the notion that it exemplified a non-Cartesian geometry called 'topological' and that this, being used to represent feed-back loops and other homeostatic systems, was a metaphor for the humanisation of science and even perhaps of society. Halley's pictures of circuitry represent, of course, neither the flow of information nor the actual circuits (whose three-dimensionality and sheer complexity might weaken his rhetoric), but rather elements of circuit diagrams of the sort that were familiar to amateur electricians in the 30s. By using such an archaic analogue he produces a striking picture, one that may imply condemnation of Mondrian as well as Stella, but at the same time he weakens his political argument. The interdependent network of a more complex cybernetic model would have been a better image of the structure of control in a society that he hopes to attack. He also weakens his argument by laying himself open to the charge of complicity twice over: that is he paints a picture which is in the first place exceptionally marketable, being assimilable by the élite as a witticism, and secondly one which is abstract in both its superficial appearance and in the sense that it overlooks the reality of its target in order to reduce it to a scheme capable of being commercialised. To the former point he may be able to reply that the enemy must be infiltrated to be subverted, but the only answer to the latter can be that no realism is possible in a radically corrupted world.

Halley's pictures were no doubt painted in complete ignorance of any British antecedents in the late 50s and early 60s, and arose in a very different global and local context. They resemble more closely some of the diagrams of control drawn and published by Steve Willats in the last 20 years, with whom Halley does share some of the same culture, that is the ideology of the New Left. In his magazine *Control,* Willats has published articles by himself and others that testify to a late, Marxist or late Socialist view of social structure, but his work is often preoccupied by the gaps in the system which allow people to create their own sub-cultures within it. He takes on some of the optimism of those who thought that the development of the cheap video camera, photocopier and offset printer in the late 60s would open up the possibilities of a participatory democracy and the by-passing of the mass media.

In the 50s, a preoccupation with semiotics flourished in the group around Hamilton, who were concerned with the phenomena of mass and international culture. The source of that concern was affection for certain of the products, rather than hatred for the class that was blamed for producing them. Nearly all the people involved were (as we would say later) 'committed' socialists and all were very well aware of the economic structure that generated their material, but they saw in their use of it a form of opposition, both to the class system as a whole and to the intellectual élitism of the mandarins and Marxists. To them it was a manifestation of working-class culture, or rather a network of interconnecting sub-cultures with which they identified themselves, demanding kinds of skill in consumption. I don't recollect that, in those optimistic days, the exact nature of the mechanisms by which the educated responses of the consumers would affect the output was fully worked out. Certainly the idea that, if one understood, one would neutralise an advertisement, either on the psychoanalytic or on the demystification (deconstruction) model, was not entertained. That would have implied the unreality of working-class ideas and desires at a time when they felt strong and did not wish to be excused for their tastes nor to be told by experts what to think and feel. Rather, it seemed to be supposed that the output of objects and images was so vast and various that individuals and particularly groups could define their identity by selecting within it. As consumers, they certainly felt that in such fields as film, advertising and packaging, the creators, sensing public response, would respond in turn by producing material that would be ever more sophisticated, couched in a form of wit playing on the knowingness of the consumer. The subsequent history of certain media, including advertising and fashion, have shown this view to be, at least to some degree, justified.

Nevertheless, for the last 20 years in Britain and for longer in France, such a view has been regarded as dangerously naive. The late Marxist criticism of Barthes is roughly contemporary with that of Alloway and Banham and shares a semiotic approach to the phenomena of mass culture. However Barthes combines a mandarin moralism with his Structuralism, onto which his followers have often grafted the recurrent continental anti-Americanism: He does not speak from inside the culture with which he often deals, but rather from that of an intellectual élite educated to rule. He is among that group of mainly French intellectuals – Sartre, Lévi-Strauss, Marcuse, Foucault, Lacan, Derrida and now Baudrillard – who, together with older figures whom they have restored to attention – Gramsci, Adorno, Benjamin etc – have been quoted everywhere in writings on art. Benjamin's elegant and passionate essay on the effect of the mass reproduction of works of art must be the most cited text of the last 10 years, especially in the United States; and yet it is a *jeu d'esprit,* having little basis in research, inaccurate in its day and falsified as a prediction. What then is the charm of such a text? One charm at least may be that though revolutionary in spirit, it deals with a matter on the fringe of fundamental matters, but close to the concerns of the art world. The belief that we no longer live in a world of objects but one of signs allows a preoccupation with the media to be redefined as the fundamental matter, with the result that an alibi for the failure of the revolutions of 1958 is achieved.

A common factor in all this writing, borrowing as it does from Marx, Freud and Saussure, is that people do not have control of what they say and, even, that they do not understand their own words. The mandarins' own texts are generally long, complex and difficult to understand. They are based on research in libraries, not in the field. The authorities cited in the footnotes are rarely ones that support the argument by substantial evidence; rather they support it by indicating a pedigree of equally insubstantiated judgements. That is to say, they exhibit the characteristics of an élite sub-culture which shows off its membership by footnotes and professional jargon, the equivalent of the fan's badge or sticker. The art writers who follow them show the same characteristics in exaggerated form.

This hostile phase of the relationship of art to the mass media is exemplified by another Englishman, a writer and an artist, Victor Burgin. His writing is full of such citations as Peter Blake's Levi jacket is of fans' badges. The message these convey is the same as that which is explicit in his text: how to be both an artist and politically committed to the Left. Alloway had called for 'descriptive study of particular aspects of the popular arts. Only after this has been done can we assess the status and role of the mass arts in our lives in the way that trigger-happy aesthetes and arm-chair educationalists are prematurely attempting'.[4] 20 years later Burgin wrote: '*we* first examine those *codes* and practices *we know de facto* to be *mass-consumed.* It is these *codes* which enshrine the *dominating ideology* and it is these *codes* which *are to be deconstructed*'.[5] The nastily authoritarian tone of this quotation is not altogether typical of Burgin, although the style is; words displaying membership of the sub-culture are in italics. Burgin's principal source for the association of semiotics and Marxism (also Freudianism) is evidently Barthes. Barthes' own mention of this issue in the first introduction to *Mythologies* (1957) is relatively unaggressive: 'I wanted to track down, in the decorative display of *what-goes-without-saying,* the ideological abuse which, in my view, is hidden there'. In the long essay at the end of this book, Barthes shows that he believes that the 'myth' can be annihilated by decypherment, but he leaves unclear the extent to which such deconstruction can be communicated to others. The principal effect of the work of what he calls the mythologist (ie demystifyer or theorist of myth) is to set himself apart. That is, he seems to take to himself the myth of the avant-garde bohemian driven by a pure moral imperative but reduced to speaking in sarcasms.

Burgin does not appear to have these doubts. Demystification or deconstruction is carried on by him as straightforward techniques of Left-committed work. If he does not imagine himself changing everyone's way of seeing, at least he is demonstrating his membership of the party. In what may be identified as his works of art as distinct from his writings, we find illustrations of his written theses: combinations of images and words constructed according to principles which, following Barthes and others, he finds in the commercial art that he believes carries bourgeois ideology. However the signs are altered by interpolations and combinations in order to deconstruct their actual or imaginary prototypes. I think that Burgin underestimates the ambivalence of his own products as a result of his own too complete identification of photography with (written) language and too great faith in the scientific validity of his sources. Since they can only be correctly interpreted as deconstructive by those who are attuned to a socio-structuralist sub-culture, they serve more to ratify a myth than to demystify it. The work of Barbara Kruger, which somewhat resembles his, carries ambiguity much further, reflecting the self-deconstruction of, I suppose, Derrida, but relying on the much greater currency, substance and urgency of feminist thought to give force to the attack.

The 70s and 80s saw the importation to the USA of many of the proponents of late Marxist ('new') art history, of Structuralist and Post-Structuralist criticism, and of their books. Their ideas have taken an ever stronger hold on the sub-cultures of art and on the mutually reinforcing courses of universities and colleges. This has taken place during a period in which there

Jeff Koons, *Pink Panther*, 1988, polychromed porcelain, 104.1 x 52.1 x 48.3 cm

Untitled, 1989, cor-ten, 300 x 50 x 25 cm

DONALD JUDD

An Interview with John Griffiths

Untitled, 1989, cor-ten, 100 x 200 x 200 cm

Recently,Waddingtons exhibited some major new pieces in metal and perspex, manufactured from the designs of Donald Judd, generally categorised as a Minimalist artist. Judd is an outspoken commentator on art and society, as revealed in his statements made in the following interview and in his critical attack, also published here, on the recent exhibition *Bilderstreit*, which attempted to confront his abstraction with the figurative painting of Baselitz.

Mr Judd, in the last two hours I have been looking at your recent works and talking to a number of interested persons: critics, historians, curators and gallery-owners. I thought it would be of value to ask you to comment on some of the points raised when the objects were, so to speak, immediate to us.

I was chatting just now with Ronald Alley, who was Keeper of the Tate Gallery's Modern Collection at the time when your work in copper there was acquired. We were studying your Waddington exhibit No 9 in cor-ten and purple plexiglass, and we both used the term 'sculptor'. But of course Mr Alley, in his catalogue of the Tate's collection, 'officially' classifies you as a sculptor. Are you a sculptor?

It depends. That's a matter of definition. I don't use the word because, literally, it's not sculpting. I think the work is three-dimensional and then it's sculpture if you think of sculpture as all work that's three-dimensional.

– But what word would you use if you needed a word to refer to it as a whole?

Then I'd say it was sculpture.

– Are you 'an artist'?

Oh yes! And sculpture's very much a part of me – fabrication.

– You're a fabricator then, but you're not a maker of myths, are you?

Oh no! No myths. Just a fabricator.

– Do your works exist apart from your works? Are they merely the evidence of concepts? When you're out of the room how do they exist for you?

I agree with Bishop Berkeley! – But yes, I think of them by now as works spread all over the world – at least, the industrialised world. And they exist inasmuch as I'm aware of them. And since I've seen a lot of other people's work, they will exist after I'm dead. Yes, like that they exist.

– Someone said: 'There are very beautiful objects, in the sense that I might say a masterpiece of Georgian furniture is very beautiful'. And someone commented: 'Yes, I agree, and, except for pieces like the 150 x 70 x 150 cm galvanised iron object, and therefore the problem of size, I can see any of these going into a very beautiful Georgian room with Georgian furniture. Any one of Judd's pieces would be an object eminently suitable for such a room.' Does that way of looking at them appeal to you? Do you agree?

That's fine by me, because I like beautiful old things. I have a certain amount of old furniture myself and it's strange, in New York on the fifth floor, though it's not Georgian but a bit later, the design is Directoire but it's Italian, I have a bench from about 1800 and that bench in its own way is about the only piece of furniture in a room with an Oldenburg, two pieces of mine and a Chamberlain and it's just fine. They all work together perfectly well. The building is 1870 so the room is 1870. Yes, it's just fine.

– What does that mean, that they work together?

It means basically that visually there's no conflict. It means a nice space you like to be in winter.

– So you don't object to people defining a work of yours as a beautiful object in a particular context?

I think it's art but it can also be a beautiful object.

– What is art as distinct from a beautiful object, with special

reference to your work?

Well, as a piece of furniture . . . well, a piece of furniture can be a beautiful object. A beautiful chair or a carpet: I got a beautiful Chi'en Mung Chinese carpet the other day. It's fabulous, it's been used: that's a beautiful object. The category of beautiful object can include art and furniture.

– Someone might pay the same sum for one of your works as for another beautiful object from another century which is described as 'art'. You don't object to the inclusion of one of your works as one among a number of beautiful 'art objects' from past and present?

No, but it's important that you call it 'art'. That distinction is important.

– How does your art now differ from early Judd?

That point seems to come up quite a bit now. I haven't thought about it a whole lot. When I started to make the work that I considered my own, in a way that was that. It would work the way it was according to whatever things I was interested in. That's I think what has happened. So the work does change. But I don't have a strong sense of . . . call it development, and I don't have any great pressure to do work. I don't have any great pressure to change, or to do something new. I'm just quite happy with it in the first place. So it's going to take its course. You know: you get older and you've things to think about and the world and lots of things, and that takes a natural course.

– Is there than a conceptual connection between your maturing experience, as this or that thing happens to you, and these particular works?

Sure there is. Yes.

– Something you can conceptualise?

Yes, you have different assumptions. You're in a different context. You have different assumptions about how long you've lived and abut how much longer you're going to have to live and all that. It's kind of a drastic thing you have to deal with, and that changes you a bit. I don't think it necessarily changes my work a great deal, but it does change it. There's also the fact that I never really expected to have any money to do anything and the possibilities now are greater than I ever imagined, because there's a lot more money to do bigger pieces and greater variety.

– Has there been any qualitative change, in texture say? Is that more important? Someone just now warned a friend not to touch one of your pieces, however lightly, because delicacy of texture, the surface bloom almost, was now so important a part of the whole.

Well, the pieces are meant to be looked at, they are not made to be touched. But if you have the pieces yourself, in your own living space, yes, though it depends what pieces, well, the present pieces are pretty tough. But if there's a whole bunch of people it becomes impossible. It's a question of quantity.

– Someone said, for instance, that you've added more colour, a lot more colour, in the last ten years. Is there some ascertainable change of that nature?

Yes, the perspexes, in one they're all red and so on. I don't think the colour's changed a whole lot, though I'm very interested in the colour, and I'd like to take it off into a certain area that I think is new to me. The Schijpol one-colour piece is an attempt to do that. I'd like to take it further. It's just a beginning. We had trouble with the factory and that stopped it. I would like to use the bright colours more. Theoretically I would consider the grey a colour, the aluminium or cor-ten is as much a colour as anything else, to me it's all colour. I had a conflict between bright colour and the nature of the material. I liked the material a great deal and perhaps colour would have to be applied and that's always been a certain conflict. Anodising is one possibility.

– But it's a problem of fabrication and not so to speak an existential choice. It just happens.

Developing the colour, you mean . . . It's an old interest which I realise is very important to me. It's an old problem. Somehow I have to find a way to get at it and at this point I don't know how to get at it. The small pieces, I think, are fine and I learned a lot from them, but the parts are small and somehow I have to learn how to make bigger printed parts and I don't quite know how to do that. Painting the metal was a problem.

– What sort of location do you conceive for your bigger pieces? Is eventual location important to you when making them?

There's a lot of different categories. Ordinarily, no. The big piece in the corner was supposed to go into a large show in Germany, but I pulled it out of the show. It's a long story.

– You can't give me a précis?

I made an agreement with the organiser that if the catalogue would include a statement by me against large shows and their implications, we would make a piece and lend it to the show. When they got the piece, first they wanted to edit it, and then they didn't want to print it. So I pulled the piece out and told them not to have any other work of mine in the show. There is work in the show, but it's over my objections.

– You're not usually thought of as an artist who makes Beuysian gestures.

I've had lots of fights for the sake of the art, but they've been more private than this one. This one's not so much a fight as that I think that big shows are really bad for art.

– Why?

Because they give the public a very strange idea about art, and in this case, as was obvious from the press releases, the show was very slanted. It was all to support Baselitz and such people.

– Do you see yourself as part of the history of Modernism?

I know that people keep using the word 'Modernism'. I'm not too sure what that means.

– It doesn't mean anything to you?

A whole lot . . . Well, what does it mean? Clem Greenberg and all those people? Actually I'm mystified by it. Is the New York School and a few people later 'Modernism'?

– Robert Hughes on TV told me the Eiffel Tower was Modernism. Do you see yourself as part of a history starting with the Eiffel Tower? It's a piece of metal, a construct and people call it art.

Sounds light talk to me. You can always say it's the end of something else and the beginning of something else.

– Do you conceive of yourself historically?

In that my work developed in a certain context, in the context of painters in New York whose work I liked a great deal, and then Barnett Newman. Always somehow I've been on the wrong side of almost everything and for some strange reason I was on the wrong side of Clement Greenberg and all those people. I'm thrown in with them when in fact they were hitting me over the head at the time. You have to talk about how things happen but it's very hard to make a really coherent history. Now no one's going around predicting anything because they don't have the faintest idea what's going to happen next. They don't know how to run a government, so five years from now . . . ?

– You're in your own history, the history of your own art?

Yes. I think it's good work; that's one thing. It's important work; but that's a social statement. And social evaluations I take with a certain amount of salt, with scepticism.

– Nevertheless, you say it.

I have to judge it from my side.

– In spite of the Greenbergs.

Criticism hasn't been too great. But actually Greenberg isn't one of the worst people. I'm not even particularly mad at the Greenbergs. Actually they made a very narrow situation out of a very big situation. I think simplification and reduction to a few categories is very bad. I think you have to argue that there is a certain kind of change; there's better change and worse change.

Untitled, 1989, plywood and plexiglass, 100 x 100 x 50 cm

In the United States right now, for example, it's changing for the worse. And it wasn't good in the first place. Reagan, Bush. To be ever more drastic, it got worse after the war.

– Has this anything to do with art?

No. There's this preposterous book which connects the course of American art after World War II with America winning the war. That's really preposterous. I really object to that.

– It is odd. But there is another book which follows up the story that in the Cold War period the CIA promoted a certain number of avant-garde artists abroad.

It's totally false. The CIA had its fingers in almost everything. I think the United States government knows very well that the artists are in opposition to it. Most public exhibitions are not of the best art. The first Russian show was Andrew Wyeth. Just this shock artist. One of the first institutional shows I was in was an exhibition in 1965 in Sao Paulo. Stella and so on; about seven artists. Barnett was the only artist who actually went, and he was sitting next to the ambassador and his wife, and she knew he was one of the artists. She said: 'Why did they send your work down here and all these other guys when they could have sent Andrew Wyeth?'

– Would you expect to see a Judd in a Gorbachev-invited show?

Maybe if Gorbachev did the show, but not if the Americans had anything to do with it. The United States is in the Brezhnev era. It's really poor, it's in bad shape.

– Do you think that in Russia they would be able to confront your work appropriately, after Wyeth?

Yes, but not with a mass show like *Bilderstreit*. That's a con. I'd like to have my own small show maybe. Or maybe with Richard Long.

– You find Long sympathetic?

A very good artist. He's probably the best. He's a real international artist. An important one.

– Like you?

A very different artist.

– Is there any other British artist you would put in the international class?

I don't think so. He's the best European artist. He's a far better artist than Bacon or Henry Moore. His work is more genuine.

– More conceptual?

I'm not interested in things that don't exist. I'm interested in things actually being done. Of course thinking goes into that. But it's not aside from that. I'm interested in the work, the thing that actually exists. What can you know about Michelangelo? What you really know is the art you see. That is the basic situation for an artist.

Above: *Untitled*, 1987, painted aluminium, 30 x 30 x 150 cm; *Centre*: *Untitled*, 1987, aluminium, green and black plexiglass, 25.4 x 25. 4 x 101.6 cm; *Below*: *Untitled*, 1987, painted aluminium, 30 x 30 x 180 cm

BILDERSTREIT

Donald Judd

It is a bad thing to imitate the bad, and not even to wish to imitate the good. (Democritus)

Very large exhibitions such as *Bilderstreit* are beneficial neither to art and artists nor to the public; they never provide a true sense of what is being done in contemporary art. Most large collections of contemporary art are not relevant, and many museum exhibitions are harmful to the work shown. Most museum collections do not represent the art of the last 40 years, even if they intend to, nor do they achieve any other purpose. Most of the activity surrounding art is not useful to it and most is harmful. Artists have very little control over their own activity, and less all the time; and strangely they don't seem to want control.

Art is by definition individual, therefore hard to sell and understand, and the purpose of most dealers during the last 40 years has been to find art that is easy to sell and to understand. Of course this subverts art and sets up a separate category of 'song and dance'. Art should be considered in the same way in which it is made; it should be thought about, decided upon, judged. Good work is not made by the shotgun approach. Vast exhibitions and collections are therefore an abrogation of responsibility, a responsibility which should be interesting.

The large exhibitions, which of course are like the art fairs, and most large collections, are part of the art business. The public and also young artists, not being able to know better, begin to think that the art business somehow has something to do with art. Commerce is not art. Education is not art. Being paid for living on art is not art. Whatever real money there is for art comes from sales in the small commercial galleries; it doesn't come from large and expensive shows. *Bilderstreit* represents the attitudes, not of the artists, but of entrepreneurial commerce. Undoubtedly it's expensive; the catalogue alone, which rapidly becomes just one of many, is expensive. Can artists get this sort of money to do their work?

This leads directly to the main economic and political issue of the time, which is that largeness is thought to be better, thought to be the goal. The large exhibitions are attempts to incorporate art into the large structures: *Bilderstreit* is the corporatising of art. These large exhibitions and collections are attempts to show that art can be institutionalised after all, that it isn't subversive; it's part of the same economic, educational and cultural system. And then what better can happen for the entrepreneurs than that the art fairs, the large exhibitions and collections actually, finally, modify art? And then where are we? The more you force art into mediocrity, the more exclusive it becomes, as its only form of protection. This is against the general relevance of good work.

To raise money for a large exhibition, there has to be an appeal to public good which, in addition to kitsch, is always their education in art; an education that is always false. They are taught the judgement of the organisers, always an attempt to be fashionable, as in *Bilderstreit*. The best work of the time is never seen as a whole. The organisers promote work they favour; they regard art as a 'scene', anything that occurs. In New York an example of this is the Whitney Biennial. How can this be education? It is unpleasant even to be in such indiscriminate and crowded rooms; its public is taught the opposite of the way art should be seen. This enforces, as the art fairs display, the idea that art is only commerce. It enforces the already strong attitude, shown in all public spaces and in architecture, that everything visual should be complicated. This desire for confusion and complication exceeds the reasons I can think of, the most obvious being that it is a sign of wealth. The large shows teach this; it's a lesson in *horror vacuii*.

Moreover, large exhibitions educate the public into believing that art is elsewhere and not in their everyday lives or in their own 'public spaces', that art is 'other', as Ortega y Gasset said. Art is something you go to see, not something you live with. It's a fashion in New York, for example, to 'gallery hop' on Saturday afternoons. The large exhibitions enforce the very strong attitude among some museum directors, collectors and dealers, especially in New York, where many of the commercial attitudes began, that the serious effort to make art by many artists is just a 'scene', one thing after the other, one 'style' after another. The point of an exhibition is usually to establish a kind of work on the 'scene'; to this end, everything is used and debased. Of course those to be established are of the moment, therefore the history of art and artists, both dead and alive, is adjustable to the negative, or to the positive if there's a resemblance. The cliches of art history, themselves questionable, are wildly used to support the argument. Art history shows its origins in commerce and uses slogans for conclusions; its clichés of influences, movements, groups and followers, even if true, are not interesting. Its superficial sociology and philosophy are used to promote the marketable and to support or criticise as needed. Having listened to quite a few sales pitches, I've concluded that both seller and buyer are capable of only two clichés, enough for the sale. It is, for example, some sort of argument that an artist has 100 followers. But these remarks are merely token selling points, token seriousness, and token reasons for big shows. Again, it's the exaltation of the periphery: the idea that everyone living from art is more interesting than the art.

Art is used to fix all that's wrong with society. It has occurred to some that diversity might be equated with democracy and that the presence of diverse styles might be used as an example of cultural virtue, allowing largeness to standardise everything else. But the large exhibitions are merely a token democracy, a falsification and subversion of real and independent activity.

There is a great deal of activity surrounding art, but little that is constructive, little with a sense of purpose. Most artists have a sense of purpose; they must have to make art. The collection of art is the only idea of most supposedly interested in art; galleries sell to collectors and museums, and together these three are the main adjuncts to art. Sometimes galleries sell art to individuals interested in art but the main criteria for collectors is to make money. However, investment depends on good judgement and a stable society, the first rare, the second doubtful, so that investment in art seems naive. Another reason is that the single work, usually a portable painting, is easily isolated from its circumstances and meaning; it becomes an easy symbol of culture and money. Involvement with art is a more complicated idea – and then there are always those damned artists.

Opportunism and self-serving in favour of one group of artists has become normal. The confused argument against the supposed determinism of the history of earlier art is normal. Invoking a new determinism to support your side is standard; so it's not surprising that *Bilderstreit* supports the work of the German Neo-Expressionists, Baselitz, Kiefer, Penck etc. There are several remarks about 'American' art in the documents; but there is no American art. Pollock, Newman, everyone denied that they were making 'American' art. I don't think even very fashionable painters like Schnabel and Salle wave the flag.

Bilder means 'painting', which doesn't mean my work or that of many others. It doesn't apply to most of the good work since the 60s, which by this title is put into an adverse position. *Bilder* also means 'image'; but for several decades no first-rate work has been an image. An image is a social product. Art, unfortunately, becomes that, but is not that. New art is new, is unknown, and cannot be an image, the product of time and familiarity. Images in art, as in much current 'Post-Modern' painting, cannot be made. Advertising can make them if you can believe them; but art has larger concerns.

The *streit*, or conflict of *Bilderstreit* is not that of artists but of the art market. There's a great tendency now for the politics and fashions of the art market to become institutionalised; the exaltation of this periphery of activity is a sign of decadence. Recently a great deal has been written about the supposed drama of the art market. If you know the situation, this is a joke. Most artists don't share or want this trivial turbulance.

The catalogue states its aim as being to present a 'panorama of visual art . . . with 1000 works of 100 important and influential artists'. Such a 'panorama' is standard now and to me horrifying and depressing, the hell of art; the quantity cannot be comprehended. There are not 100 first-rate artists and many will not be in this exhibition anyway. Another of its stated aims is to 'examine the tensions between the "older" generation and young artists of today, especially emphasising contemporary works that can be conceived of as quotations and fragments'. These are virtually slogans, and 'quotations' simply appeals to the freedom to be unfree. The secret is that the artists supported are very unimaginative, very dull, very academic and ripe for institutionalisation. Their absence of imagination must be justified, hence it is alright to 'quote' earlier work, which is merely copying, debasing the work of others.

This exhibition is for a few painters but the text is for all artists. Many of those who live off art and many who buy it seem to resent art. This is a growing attitude and a strange one. I think partly it is a resentment of seriousness and independence, partly the attitude of patronage. Perhaps now that I've written this, we will find out if *streit* can occur at home!

Untitled, 1989, galvanised iron, 150 x 750 x 150 x cm

NANCY SPERO

Sky Goddess II, 1986, handprinting collage/handprinting on paper, 61 x 9.14 cm

I try to challenge the prevailing standards of the male 'gaze' – the way in which women are coerced culturally and physically. Some of my recent work expresses exuberance – a sense of possibility and self-assertion, control over one's body in a world not male-controlled. A sort of utopia, of change. On the other hand, the work you see on the floor is about pain, about total destruction and disintegration. The female figures are like negatives or shadows. Iridescent as they run or mourn over the landscape of broken bodies. They are irradiated with the poison of modern destruction – even Artemis 'who heals woman's pain' is irradiated. I deal with both poles of women's experience.

Artist's statement, 1987, New York City

Nancy Spero's task of reclaiming women's history in her art must be seen as an integral part of her long-standing involvement in activist causes for political and social change . . .
Resisting easy codification, Spero's art gives definition to her experience as a woman and activist artist and on the margin of acceptability. Her technique involves the use of the long tablet format, derived from Medieval manuscripts and the Egyptian *Book of the Dead*, on which collaged or stamped images are juxtaposed with verbal signs and blank spaces. Such formats, borrowed from sources as diverse as cinema and poster techniques, allow Spero the flexibility to express a range of concerns and emotions.

Spero's scrolls that contain repeatedly stamped, generic images of women from different cultures throughout history defy the concept of authenticity, while the anti-hierarchical reading subverts a 'heroic' or 'monumental' impulse. The printing technique of repetition emphasises flux, as one image can look different when repeated since the record of change is inherent in the process. Such work is intentionally contradictory: it is delicate yet ambitious, intimate yet remote, stable yet dislocated. This mutability enables Nancy Spero to create perfect structures for her art. Here time is a continuum that contains the pain/pleasure of the world of sexual relation that grounds everything, uprooting all that is not itself.

Dominique Nahas

If Spero's earlier works focused on women's pain, the later works body forth woman's pleasure and her potential. The scrolls now extend vertically as well as horizontally, the large expanses of white, the silences in the earlier scrolls, are now filled with lush colour and the texts seem to have been replaced by larger, more sensual female bodies. As Lisa Tickner describes it, we enter a world where 'naked women are unmolested; sprinting women are never tripped; laughing women remain ungagged. The image is one of freedom from every kind of physical, mental and social constraint; a freedom we do not possess but need to nurture, as an idea or a feeling, as our talisman against the oppression of habit, the grind of everyday obligation and normality'. Spero has always been out of place, out of time, painting dark expressionist canvases during the minimalist years, and now when expressionist painting has returned and male artists are making what she refers to as 'big splats', she is assembling fragile prints on paper, little things 'with bite'. She intends to stay out of place. . . 'I wanted to depict women finding their voices, which partly reflected my own developing dialogue with the art world . . . I'm speaking of equality, and about a certain kind of power of movement in the world, and yet I'm not offering any systematic solutions'.

Jo-Anna Isaak, *Nancy Spero: Works Since 1950*
Everson Museum of Art, Syracuse, New York, 1987

Above: *Three Seated Black Women*, 1987, acrylic, 304.8 x 408.9 cm; *Below*: *Four Black Men*, 1985, acrylic, 304.8 x 485.2 cm

LEON GOLUB

Peter Schjeldahl

Yellow Sphinx, 1988, acrylic, 304.8 x 378.5 cm

The improbable late flowering of Leon Golub, as a political artist who is also one of the major painters of our time, continues apace. The new paintings are among his best, lacking none of the disturbing power of his earlier *Mercenaries* and *Interrogations* while showing gains in fluency, formal invention, and complexity of meaning. Their sheer quantity is part of the good news. After years of toiling alone with an exhausting technique, Golub now has assistants for such rote chores as the endless scraping down that gives his pictures their extraordinary surface quality; he has thereby attained what is for him the breakneck production rate of a half-dozen or so paintings a year. In terms of public reception, meanwhile, the new work seems sure to accelerate, if only a little, Golub's assumption of a deserved central position in contemporary art – not that resistance to him will ever collapse in a culture where the term 'political art' is either repressive dismissal or debilitating loyalty oath. Too raw for some and too ambiguous for others, his art gives scant comfort to partisans of any stripe, who – along with those of escapist taste – may prefer to give these pictures a wide berth.

Viewers who do risk a confrontation with Golub's new work will have little doubt that it is by a great artist of harrowing portents: a 'Conradian painter', as Gerald Marzorati has finely called him, who envisions the ways of power 'upriver, where the wires fray'. The comparison is shaded by an important irony: our time is not that of Joseph Conrad, when the *Heart of Darkness* lay beyond the supposed light of civilisation. Today darkness and light are weirdly mixed, even interchangeable, in Third World situations where barbarity at the fringe performs workaday service for the interests of the centre. Golub insists that we admit our brotherhood with evil-doers who act in proxy for the maintenance of our privileges, and he has now begun to insist further, in his stunning paintings of less-than-friendly African blacks, that we see our complicity beamed at us through the eyes of its victims – or *former* victims, perhaps, whom long abuse has ominously toughened. There must be no equivocation about the revolutionary sympathies of Golub's stance.

At the same time, an attentive viewer of Golub's art will immediately sense the inadequacy of any narrowly political interpretation of the paintings, which are drastically over-qualified for the menial labour of propagandising. Golub makes no secret of his politics, but neither does he advertise or impose them. His art isn't a programme to be joined but a set of truths to be assimilated, truths about the 'out there' of objective criminality but also about the 'in here' of subjective ambivalence. Like Conrad, Golub is drawn to 'the fascination of the abomination', the dirty secrets of the soul. He is a political artist in that he requires real correlatives, in the world of human action – not for him the harmless acting-out of expressionistic fantasy – however in confessing that he can imagine not just the fact but the very bliss of evil he abrogates the ideologue's cherished right to be righteous. Golub's transcending allegiance to art's revealing and redeeming power, a power fundamentally indifferent to questions of right and wrong and action and inaction, makes him at once a dubious cadre and an artist worthy of the highest comparison, which in this case means Goya.

An imaginative capacity to penetrate, and in some way to share, the pathos of violence is common to the few great artists whose work has been overtly political. Goya let the cat out of the bag in his incredible 'Black Paintings', made on the walls of his house strictly for (one may say with awe) his own amusement: Malignity's horrific glee is there distilled for all time, a truth beyond the reach of nearly all other creative minds – even Picasso's. It is instructive to note how, in his own attempts at

Above: *White Squad IX*, 1985, acrylic, 304.8 x 365.8 cm; *Below*: *Prisoners I*, 1985, acrylic, 304.8 x 434.3 cm

political statement, Picasso is regularly way-laid by an obviously unexplored affinity to the criminal: his marvellous drawings of Franco, motivated by hatred, backfire by making the tyrant an intensely appealing little demon, Ubu Roi redux. A decade ago, when Golub, at the lowest point in his career, came to make pictures of Franco and other wielders of power, he did them absolutely deadpan, with no emotion save that of wondering scrutiny – as if to say, 'Who is this guy?' Unlike Picasso and like Goya, Golub was then able to proceed to the heart of the matter: 'Who (and *what*) is anybody (me included)?'

It is a question that in Golub's beautiful and alarming new paintings *Four Black Men* and *Four Blacks* calls for a quick answer. These pictures enact moments of intrusion, and it is we, the viewers, who have intruded. We are aware less of seeing than of being seen: being instantly judged in ways that threaten to vacate our own senses of ourselves. This is a theatrical effect, like most of the major tropes in art today. What makes it uniquely Golub's is its reliance on a fantastic specificity of characterisation. Like no other current painter except, perhaps, Eric Fischl, Golub gives living reality to *others* – people presented in relation to the viewer on terms that are entirely their own. His fictional blacks are larger than life in every way, instantly familiar as individuals and all the more mysterious as a result. We feel the pressure in their expressions and gestures, their clothes and demeanor, of whole lifetimes of experience that, at this moment, provide the principles by which we are being sized up. A realisation slowly dawns: we, too, are a fictional character in this painting, our role projected on to us through all those eyes.

The sense of being anticipated and included in what is shown, of being made a self-conscious participant, is as basic to Golub's art as it is to theatre. Again like (good) theatre, Golub marshals all his illusions – and anti-illusions, in the Brechtian vein of heightening artifice by rendering it flat-footedly patent – toward a single effect of engagement. Though shadowless, Golub's pictures are cunningly lighted in the way their colours and textures at once soak up actual, gallery light and convey the air and temperature, the humidity and smell, of their fictive ambiences. Critics often remark on his uncanny way with the grunginess of worn and soiled clothing, but it is only the most obvious of his devices. (I attribute its special aesthetic piquancy to the fact of pigment scraped into the canvas fabric: dirty cloth representing dirty cloth!) His knack for getting the indeterminate translucency of flesh is even more remarkable. At present he is making strong progress against his one chronic formal problem, that of backgrounds which have tended to be inert and to seem arbitrary. The moodily luminous white cinderblock walls in the paintings of blacks, the De Chirico-esque space and dream-flavoured mint and forest greens in *Riot VI*, and especially the motif of colonial-classic architecture in *White Squad IX* all contribute 'characters' of their own to the dramatic proceedings.

White Squad IX stands in useful contrast to the black paintings, exemplifying an opposite pole of Golub's theatrical repertoire. This is not a picture that looks out at us, but one that we look in on – with some frustration, in this case, because the two white figures block our view of what is happening to the felled black man. Not knowing, we can't be sure of the meaning of the black squad-member's expostulation: Is he advising or pleading? The picture's architectural background, meanwhile, gives important information. Clearly we are in a main square of some city or town (most likely a town, given the black's fieldhand garb and the bald white man's riding clothes), so this is no back-alley violence but something occurring in full public view. We may be seeing only a fragment of a panoramic event, a riot or mass round-up. Imagining this, I have a ghostly sense of commotion behind and around me as I look at the painting. What's my role? The three captors have their backs trustingly turned to me, so I must be an ally. I feel that I know these men, almost to the point of knowing their names. I don't like them – the hired black irregular, the gross and jodhpured country squire, and the seasoned thug in military cap and shoes – but then, they may not like me much, either. We are comrades, thick as thieves, in a cause which does not require that we like each other.

Golub's inwardly focused pictures tend to do this to you, getting you to play a fantasy role in a high old time of manly mayhem. But the role is never quite the same in any two paintings. In *Prisoners I*, it is not at all clear that we are one of the boys with the snarling brute of a soldier. In fact – as evidence of a present shift of Golub's prime identification away from torturers toward their victims – we are apt to be one of the prisoners in this horrible shuttered room where the time (by the soldier's watch, which is hiked up his arm to protect it, perhaps, from damage) looks to be 2.20, maybe in the afternoon but somehow probably in the morning. The way the soldier is proportioned, his shoe twice the size of his head, suggests the perspective of someone on the floor. The two depicted prisoners are at eye-level with us. The black one is in a paroxysm of pain or fear. The light-skinned one (an old Indian?) is glazed and vacant, as if his soul were in refuge somewhere far away. How are *we* taking it? Racking my own memory for parallel experiences – being beaten up as a kid, being mugged as an adult – I find their total well short of the terror I would feel on this occasion. I don't know how I would take it. Being a white middle-class American, I will surely never find out.

Golub is a master choreographer of the male body in violence. The heavy pivot of the soldier measuring his punch in *Prisoners I* is rather beautiful, and note the delicate tension in his left hand. (Golub garners a lot of subtle poetry from the unconscious disposition of one hand while the other hand is engaged in conscious action: See especially *White Squad IX*, where unused hands provide our only clue to what is being done.) A likeness to dance is quite delirious in *Riot IV*'s figure with a rope. He bends knees, shifts hips, and dips shoulders to tug zestfully at the victim of, perhaps, his buddy's club. The buddy has got to be one of the most perfectly nightmarish figures in art, a creature of antic malevolence whose slack-jawed head, expressing his forward rush, seems to grow from his chest. He has us in his sights, it appears. Or does he? Observe that both men are left-handed, an odd coincidence – unless *we* are the club-wielder and are glimpsing, with boundless satisfaction, our own reflection, perhaps in a shop window.

There is no need to decide such things one way or another, because Golub purposely leaves them open to variable interpretation. Each viewer is free to make his or her own story about the paintings – but not free to have *no* story. Golub will not tolerate the self-distancing of connoisseurship, which he takes pains to defeat. A good part of his formal brilliance is devoted to rupturing aesthetic unity: unstretched canvas and brusque cropping serve this negative end. He makes paintings for use, not for admiration. Their function is to aid in the getting of knowledge, about both world and self, by willing souls. Though vast and frontal, Golub's paintings are peculiarly passive in their address, disdaining to grab viewers by the throat. Rather, they wait. They hold their secrets in trust for those who will feel a need for them. They have a lovely tact, a civility. Unlike the usual run of 'protest art', they do not react to brutality by following its example; instead, they stare it down. By way of open-ended narrative, thoroughly at the service of the viewer's imagination, they lead to moral empowerment, the sombre joy of knowing the worst – not abstractly but in one's own vulnerable person, one's own share of the common humanity that hangs by a breakable thread of decency. Golub adds strength to the thread.

SOL LEWITT
Wall Drawings

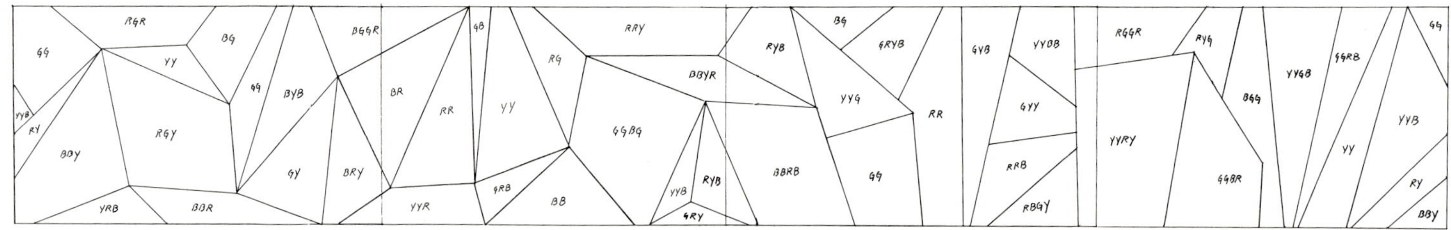

On four walls, continuous forms with colour ink washes superimposed

Colour ink wash.
First Drawn by: Antoine Bonhomme, Fransje Killaars, Anthony Sansotta, Roy Villevoye.
First installation: Chateau d'Oiron, Oiron, France, August 1987.
Collection: Yvon Lambert, Paris, France.
First and third walls:
560 x 920 cm
Second and fourth walls:
560 x 920 cm.

In a continuing series of installations throughout Europe and the USA, Sol LeWitt 'used the surface of a wall as just another support for a drawing, basically in an analogy to a sheet of drawing paper . . . According to LeWitt, the main point of drawing immediately onto a wall was to achieve the greatest possible two-dimensionality of a drawing. To draw onto a wall, to inscribe the wall with lines, appeared to be one way of avoiding any illusion . . . instead of drawing on paper behind glass in a frame on a wall there would simply be a drawing on a wall . . . the Wall Drawings have always been con-

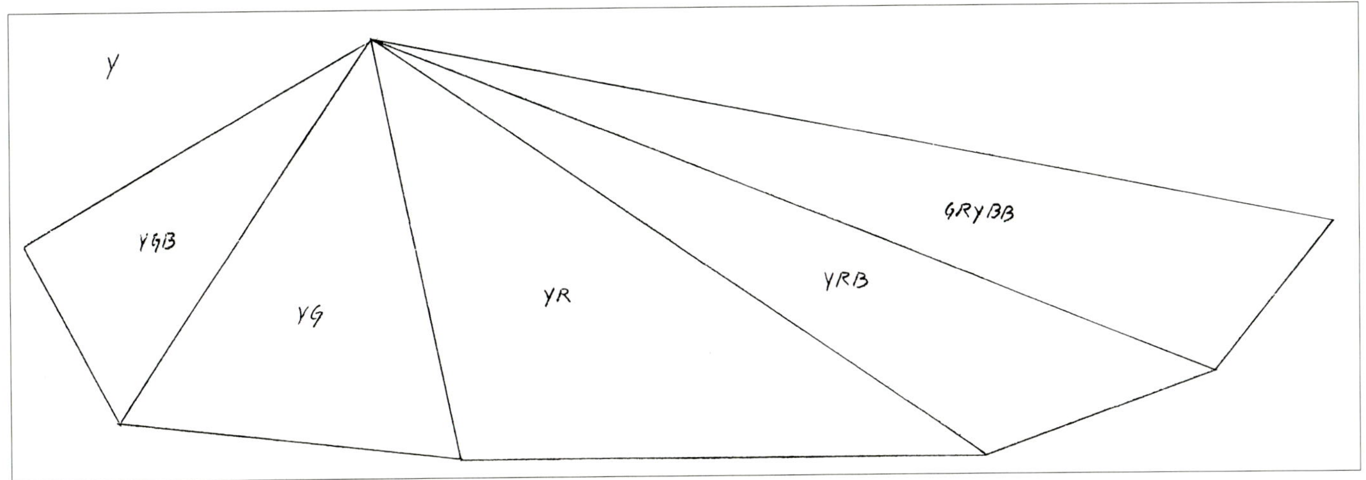

-ceived as autonomous. . . At the same time, the concept of a Wall Drawing implies its own non-exclusivity by introducing – on the perceptual level – the wall, part of that 'reality' that is not art . . . Sol LeWitt's art exploits those artistic possibilities that mutually subvert the dichotomy of conception and perception and that result from the collapse of this dichotomy.' (Ulrich Loock, *Sol LeWitt Wall Drawings 1984-88*, Kunsthalle Bern 1989)

This brief presentation of Sol LeWitt's recent projects coincides with the exhibition at the Lisson Gallery in London.

Asymmetrical pyramid with colour ink washes superimposed

Colour ink wash. The apex is left. The background is yellow. Five sides. 1 – yellow, grey, blue; 2 – yellow, grey; 3 – yellow, red; 4 –yellow, red, blue; 5 – grey, red, yellow, blue, blue.

First Drawn by: David Higginbotham, Anthony Sansotta, Jo Watanabe.

First installation: Brooklyn Museum, Brooklyn, NY, May 1985.

Collection: Eva LeWitt, Chester, CT. 600 x 1800 cm.

Above: *Untitled (Large Christ)*, 1987, silver print, tape, film, glass, wood, 228.6 x 609.6 cm; *Below*: *Nipple*, 1987, silver print, tape, 177.8 x 254 cm

DOUG & MIKE STARN

Triple Luther Detail, 1985-9, toned silver print, tape, glue, wood, glass, 187.9 x 175.2 cm

While walking through the Louvre in Paris on an art school trip in March of 1985, Doug and Mike Starn passed through room after room of dramatic, Counter-Reformation imagery – crucifixions, martyrdoms, ascensions, and miraculous events, most rendered in a style that placed a premium on physical and emotional intensity. Philippe de Champaigne's *Le Christ mort (Dead Christ)*, a 23 x 77-inch, mid-17th century oil on panel, was, for them, a halcyon amidst the tumult of Rubens, Jordaens, Guercino, and Pietro da Cortona. Drawn to the calm and gentle melancholy of this work, the Starns photographed it. The negative has since generated a body of works, all relatively similar in mood although often quite different in form. About 25 of these pieces have been selected by the Starns for an installation of their own design at the John and Mable Ringling Museum of Art –*The Christ Series*.

These are not appropriation photographs designed to deconstruct – or expose – the context in which the original art was made. The device of isolating the motif and pushing it to the foreground makes it function as an emblem. The object seems drained of its original significance; the fact that it is Christ as opposed to any dead figure seems secondary.

The first work the viewer sees is *Untitled (Large Christ)*, 1987, a 6 x 188-ft image of the Saviour. Toned blue, He takes on the chilling pallor of death. Above His legs, the artists have placed a photograph of an endless sea, represented by just water, sky, and horizon line. This emblem of infinity is reinforced by toning this photograph a light brown; contrasting it with the black ground on which it sits, functioning like a window punched in the surface of the work through which a golden, divine light emanates.

The Starns, through their emphasis on the physicality of the medium, have ruptured the smooth taut surface of the photographic image. The surface no longer functions as a window through which we see. Since the invention of photography, much of the magic of the medium lay in its ability to convince us of its link to a real moment. When we look intently at a photograph, we can find ourselves immersed in the scene represented, we can forget we are looking only at a photograph, and we can lose awareness, becoming mentally transported to the world in the photograph. In a Starns print, the illusion must struggle to exist. The medium has the greater reality, and by calling so much attention to the artifacts of the medium, the artificiality of the image is exposed. The subject is distanced from us – the reality of the original scene recorded by the camera is further removed.

The Starns further distance the image by fragmenting it. Since a work of theirs is generally made up of many prints taped together, the underlying image is contiguous rather than continuous, even when the prints are aligned to allow for a relatively cohesive reading. The Starns emphasise the edge of the paper: tape highlights the shape of each component print, and adjoining prints often vary, toned darker or lighter or different colours. The geometric pattern of the paper runs through, and thus becomes part of, the image. The Starns' works are a photographic Cubism, with the geometric patterning of the individual sheets of paper fracturing and distancing the underlying "picture" in much the same way that the lambent planes of an Analytic Cubist painting veil and jostle a representational world that supposedly lies beneath. But, of course, the world denied by the geometric patterning in a Starns photograph was at one time a real world, not an illusionistic one as in a painting. This is no small distinction, since it is this melting away of reality that makes the Starns' work so compelling.

Doug & Mike Starn: Projects 1
The John & Mable Ringling Museum of Art, Sarasota, Florida

Jane Hammond, *Untitled*, 1988, oil on birch ply, 186.2 x 171.5 cm. The paintings of Jane Hammond are synthesised by a random selection of images from a 'vocabulary' of 276 'pieces of information' which she has collected from various sources – children's drawings, mathematics, alchemical symbols, biology, cultural anthropology and so forth. By selecting and recombining them she allows for certain loose associations without embuing specific meaning. 'Context is everything when trying to create meaning', says Hammond. 'Put a cowboy next to a pin-up girl and its about gender. Put the same cowboy next to a cactus and its about the old west'. Thus all of the works are untitled so as not to give clues or false presumptions of meaning.

EXIT ART

Papo Colo, *Discourse the Invention of Dynamics*, 1987-8, 127 x 182.8 cm. Colo has said, 'To be an exile, an immigrant, is to believe that you belong. My art is of the spirit that doesn't belong . . . sometimes I believe that my art is the search for belonging.'

EXIT ART, founded in 1982 by Jeanette Ingberman and Papo Colo, and situated on Broadway, is an art organisation concerned with exploring multi-cultural, multi-disciplinary issues in contemporary art through critical presentations and publications. Concerned with 'The right of culture to change itself' and 'The right of history to have opinions', the purpose of EXIT ART is outlined as follows:

– to provide a context for understanding the art of the Americas as we approach a new definition of our continent through an appreciation of the transcultural changes and challenges occurring in our society.

– to provide a different historical perspective on the culture by establishing a substantial dialogue among diverse backgrounds and aesthetic values in contemporary art.

– to organise comprehensive one-person shows of mid-career artists who have not received critical attention or exposure and through catalogues with critical essays to place their work in an historical context.

– to educate the community in the diversity of art realities: the parallel histories which exist in our contemporary culture.

– to document artists whoseworks are difficult to categorise or exhibit either because of their content or manner of working, and to make this information available to a larger public through exhibitions and publications.

– to work with individual artists to sponsor and produce special projects including: installations, record albums, print portfolios, performances, films, special edition books, etc.

Juan Sánchez, *Mixed Statement*, 1984, oil, photo-collage, mixed media, 140 x 240 cm. A Pueto-Rican artist born in Brooklyn, Sánchez confronts the political and religious issues particularly affecting his community.

Martin Wong, *Untitled*, 1988, installation view, Exit Art. Wong's own cultural displacement (as San Francisco-born Chinese), has led him to produce art that represents his social, political and individual conditions, and those of other culturally isolated groups, especially Afro-Americans and Hispanics. His paintings depict simplified but meticulous details of every brick or scrap of graffiti in his chosen world. 'The real action for Wong is in the streets. In the spirit of graffiti, he displays an affection for and familiarity with public spaces, walls, seemingly abandoned buildings, and locked gates, which are ominous, but not insurmountable.' (Elisabeth Hess)

David Hammons, *Untitled*, 1989, installation view, Exit Art. Environmental sculptor and performance artist, Hammonds produces works that are not normally confined to a gallery space. This piece pays hommage to images of the railroad inherent in much of the music and many of the artifacts of Afro-American culture. It is a vision of life on 'the wrong side of the tracks' utilising the songs of John Coltrane, James Brown and Thelodius Monk, together with a length of rail track, electric trains, coal, 15 grand piano tops and a wheel of Night Train Express bottles. Hammond's interest lies in the depiction of human richness and suffering rather than the making of trite ideological statements.

Anton van Dalen, *Auto Aviary*, 1988, wood, wire and live pidgeons, 198 x 426.7 x 121.9 cm, installation view, Exit Art. This work combines two of the artist's obsessions – the pidgeon and the car – creating a powerful metaphor. Van Dalen combines in his work the roles of artist and naturalist. He incorporates his love of nature (in particular birds), with portrayal of the urban jungle in which he dwells. 'If you see how artists live, the way they live becomes their world . . . I grew up in Holland . . . and spent a lot of time running through the woods, along the rivers, the canals.' He saw the car partly as a mechanical bird, but also as the symbol of American culture and urbanisation. His art seeks to highlight and conversely to erode the dichotomy between these symbols.

Ursula von Rydingsvard, *Untitled*, 1988, cedar and graphite, 157.4 x 510.4 x 106.6 cm, installation view, Exit Art. Van Rydingsvard works entirely in wood, starting with vast naked blocks and hacking away to find the forms within, reminiscent of barracks, coffins and pitchforks. Despite the recollection of childhood trauma, of time spent in a forced labour camp in Germany, she rejects a Kafkaesque reading of her work, refusing to see herself as a victim. 'My view is more like that of the person in the corner who watches or senses. One of the things I would be most ashamed of is pathos in my work. Or to have blatant pain, like the kind Francis Bacon puts in his paintings. I want this kind of packed pride, this containment of emotions – like Giotto.'

THE ALTERNATIVE MUSEUM

The Social and Political Responsibilities

Geno Rodriguez (from an interview with Roger Denson)

Mundy McLaughlin, *Freedom*, 1985, cibacrome colour photograph, 40.6 x 50.8 cm

The Alternative Museum is the first museum of contemporary art founded and operated by artists in the history of the United States and the only one dedicated to art with a socio-political content. I wanted to demonstrate that museums could be established by artists themselves, not just by very affluent individuals such as Guggenheim, Getty etc, and that the average person can become responsible for his or her own socio-political environment.

I believe the general public thinks of museums primarily as warehouses and showcases for works of art. We are taught to believe that this is the sole responsibility of a museum, and that museums exist as a form of élite entertainment for the educated, for those who have studied art and art-history courses. But people forget that museums also have a tremendous social responsibility. Such responsibilities tend to be put aside, because many of the relevant socio-political issues are disturbing to staff members who have to stimulate public dollar support from people who might disapprove of issue-oriented presentations.

Education is the primary role of the museum; staff must therefore become more responsible in selecting exhibitions and not merely succumb to predominating tastes. For example, museums which interact with the art world tend to pander to the tastes of collectors, dealers, critics and artists who are thought to be in vogue; if a painter becomes popular, everyone wants to show him. I don't find many museums giving the public what they don't expect to see, or what they don't already know from visiting commercial galleries. Such a museum would never show an exhibition which contains provocative content which sectors of the public would rather not know about. This attitude is not an example of social responsibility on the part of a museum.

New museums should have opinions, for by presenting exhibitions with an opinion, dialogue is created. Moreover, museums have another responsibility – it's called leadership. But to lead one must really believe in something.

Most museum exhibitions are oriented solely toward the dominant American culture with the implication that other Americans of non-European descent must adapt their interest to the main cultural group. Social responsibility in this case means equality in consideration and presentation. It also means going out of your way to understand the needs of all the American people.

When I say 'social' I have to include 'political'; and indeed the economic as well. There are many exhibitions that could confront socio-political issues – religion, sexuality, morality, poverty, economics, politics – but other museums refuse to handle such content.

Although we are dedicated to contemporary artists, I think of the relation as a partnership. On the other hand, if there were no museums, there would probably be a lot fewer artists. Artists do not work in a vacuum; they must have walls on which to hang work. And since commercial galleries are more about commerce, the artist does need a place in which to explore new ideas.

The Alternative Museum devotes itself in particular to mid-career artists. With the young artists commanding more and more attention, the older artists were stopped in their tracks by economic factors and lack of recognition; they were left out. The Alternative Museum took on the responsibility of bringing these artists back into the spotlight, devoting a catalogue to discussing their career – past, present and future. Likewise, there are a number of artists making work with strong political content who were unable to find a serious space in which to exhibit. We decided that someone had to provide a forum for this work and we became recognised for assembling exhibitions which have a strong socio-political content. Everyone else wants to show the Meyer Vaismans and the Cindy Shermans, but we don't . . .

ARTIST'S SPACE
Linda Cathcart

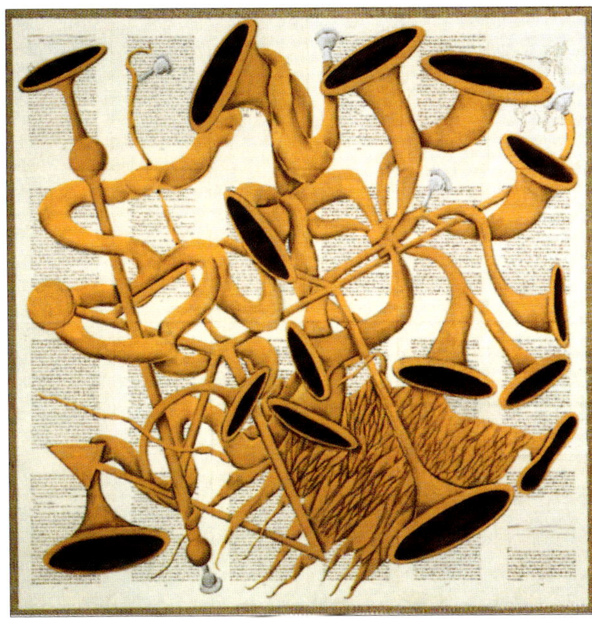

L to R: Jonathan Kessler, *Parasite*, 1984, mixed media construction with lights and motors, 111.8 x 119.3 x 58.4 cm; Tim Rollins & KOS, *The Nature Theater of Oklahoma VI*, 1986, oil and china markers on book pages, *Amerika* by Franz Kafka, 81.3 x 81.3 cm

Artist's Space, an exhibition space conceived in 1973 as an alternative to the commercial gallery, was created to expose the work of unaffiliated artists, and to enable a more radical, New York-based art scene to develop. Concerned with 'the activity of art itself' rather than with defining a political stance, Artist's Space has played a significant role in art of the 80s, exhibiting the early work of, among others, Koons, Salle, Holzer and Kruger.

Artistically, the era between 1973 and 1983 was characterised by the idea that there were many kinds of art being made, experimentation in many forms, but no single predominant style. There was a feeling of dissatisfaction combined with anticipation as to what ideas would become the most appropriate and expressive and which would characterise contemporary art. Artist's Space had a definite hand in creating the situation and crystalising ideas that were to become the identity of art of the 80s.

At the inception of Artist's Space, the existence and purpose of alternative spaces were only beginning to be recognised. Seemingly, they had come about in response to the relative inactivity of new art; alternative spaces were founded mainly by artists for places to exhibit their own works and those of other artists they admired. In New York, some Soho area galleries featured the work of younger artists, but most were showing the work of nationally or internationally-known artists. This situation provided a dramatic backdrop for the artists exhibiting at Artist's Space, throwing their efforts into high relief, so that a more radical, New York based scene could develop. Artist's Space itself has never functioned as a meeting place for artists on a day-to-day basis, but it has functioned as a place where multidisciplinary activity could take place. It has never evinced a political position or any philosophical cant, but rather is surprisingly democratic and is only devoted to the activity of art itself. The significance of Artist's Space has extended beyond any of the separate discuplines it encouraged. It has supported painting, sculpture, music, dance, film and performance art. It has provided an atmosphere which encouraged artists to take chances and to realise ideas – to create what seemes almost impossible.

Artist's Space is not easily categorised. It is not a funky-anything-goes space. It does not take an anti-materialist stand. It is not aggressive. It is not angry. It is simply alternative. Interestingly enough, the work exhibited in it does not come out of nowhere, it has presedence, like all interesting art does and those precedents are somewhat easier to trace at Artist's Space than perhaps at other alternative spaces because of the oiginal artists-nominating-artists policy. Often the older artists would nominate their students or someone who had come to their attention through apprenticeship. Looking at this relationship gives us some idea of the stimulus and historical perspective affecting these young artists. The artists who began to show at Artist's Space in the mid-70s were not artists who belonged to the traditions of the 60s. They were not Pop artists, they were not Minimalist, they were not necessarily conceptual artists. They were artists who wanted to make art in the spaces between these definitions and they wanted urgently to have a place to exhibit it. These artists who exhibited here were mostly products of training in other American cities during the late 60s and early 70s. They grew up with the attitudes that they had learned in school toward using traditional media and realism or Abstract Expressionism or hard-edged painting of some sort. They also were looking at the recent work of the process-oriented, anti-aesthetic, post-minimal artists who were using new materials. It was the latter of this group which seems to have mostly inspired artists showing at Artist's Space to work directly using installations and then subsequently with images taken from the media.

Julian Schnabel, *Resurrection: Albert Finney Meets Malcolm Lowry*, 1984, oil and modelling paste on velvet, 25.4 x 9.5 cm, courtesy Pace Gallery

JULIAN SCHNABEL
Mannerist Impressario of the Apocalypse

Donald Kuspit

Julian Schnabel, *King of the Wood*, 1984, oil and bondo with plates and bronze casting of spruce roots on wood, 25.4 x 49.5 cm, courtesy Pace Gallery New York

DK: *Picasso once said that what engages us in Cézanne is his anxiety. Do you think it is your anxiety – very different from Cézanne's – that engages the spectator subliminally, and finally wells up and overpowers him or her?*
JS: *I don't know, but I'd rather call it anxiousness, the sense that things aren't right. I want to put something in the world that can communicate this in a concentrated, shorthand way, that finally becomes explosive. Such a thing simultaneously destroys and saves you through its constant anxiousness.*

Julian Schnabel in an interview with the author, Nov 1987

Julian Schnabel is usually described as a Post-Modernist artist: his works are full of the flotsam and jetsam of history, particularly the history of suffering. This is true from *Jack the Bellboy 'A Season in Hell'*, 1975, in which Schnabel identifies with Rimbaud, to *King of the Wood* and *Resurrection: Albert Finney Meets Malcolm Lowry*, both 1984, and beyond, to the group of works called *Stations of the Cross*, 1986-7, which include works dealing with St Ignatius of Loyola and the death of Joseph Beuys. In all these works Schnabel eagerly embraces and excavates the death that has been foretold, that has been pre-figured and pre-pictured in a thousand and one narratives and images. He eagerly identifies with a destiny of pain – with the heart, that *Afflicted Organ*, to allude to a 1987 work.[1] His is an eschatological art, appropriating the master meanings of life and the master languages of art to reassert the sense of hurt and loss that pervades both.

Schnabel draws from a wealth of visual sources, both high art and popular culture, as has become the Post-Modernist habit. Traces of Antique, Renaissance, Baroque, and Modern sources – residues of residues, the dregs of the collective art memory – are found in his art, ranging from various broken Classical statues to paintings by Pollaiuolo, El Greco, Goya, Max Beckmann, among many others.[2] In the 80s, all styles and images have come to be regarded as equally valid, equally available. And Schnabel has mined them for all they are worth, indeed, performed a kind of reverse mining, in which the refined style and image is transformed back into raw ore. He reverses the alchemical art process, going from gold to lead, forfeiting light for darkness, the transcendental for the fatal, the sublime for deadweight. Or rather, he is shipwrecked on the boundary between the opposites. In a fresh primitivism, he returns sophisticated style and image to their archaic roots.

This is part of his mannerist anti-classicism, further in evidence in his mode of composition, where he frequently jams various archaicised sources together, seemingly overloading the picture. They exist side by side, so many juxtaposed and jumbled fragments, jarring in their discontinuity. *Prehistory: Glory, Honor, Privilege, Poverty*, 1981, is a particularly triumphant example. A pictorial unity of sorts emerges, a mosaic unity, which is mannerist in import. It is an archaic unity, one that barely holds, a nominal unity, a unity that is integrative and disintegrative at once, an insecure unity that suggests the insecurity of the archaic self – the fragmented, crumbled state of a self that desperately clings to its grandiosity.

The mosaic character of Schnabel's work is self-evident in his plate paintings, but he uses a mannerist mode of composition generally, carrying it to an extreme. That is, in Arnold Hauser's words, he abandons 'the fiction that a work of art is an organic, indivisible, and unalterable whole, made all of a piece'. He 'aspires to richness, multiplicity, variety, and exquisiteness'.[3] Strange as it may sound, his archaicising strategy is a way of making his sources psychologically exquisite.

Like a good mannerist composition, Schnabel's composition has 'no centre anywhere' and, indeed, actively asserts its lack of centre. Certain figures may be featured, but they are torn apart – broken or crumbled, as though on a rack or in a meat grinder – by their mannerist handling. The parts of Schnabel's picture never fit together, comfortably adapt to one another, and can't be made to do so: 'a mannerist work is not so much a picture of reality as a collection of contributions to such a picture'. In Schnabel's case, these contributions are already at the remove of art, belong to the zone of art, where, as Freud said, the narcissistic pleasure principle has transformed reality so that it is less traumatic. Schnabel's archaicising of these artistic contributions brings them closer to psychological reality, especially the reality of anxiousness. In fact, mannerist composition exists to articulate and monitor anxiousness – perhaps the most archaic of emotional states – like a seismograph. Anxiousness is an inner malaise always waiting to become an outer catastrophe – an explosion, as Schnabel says. His works convey it both as a latent threat and a disastrous reality.

Hauser describes the mannerist composition as 'a labyrinth you lose yourself in, and do not seek to escape from' because you know you can't – a labyrinth of anxiousness, one might add. The strong sense of incompleteness or irresolution – also typically mannerist – that pervades Schnabel's compositions, and that accompanies the sense of inescapability and endlessness conveyed by a labyrinth, correlates with anxiousness. Indeed, it implies the failure of any attempt at completeness, self-containment, that is, of making things and the self right.

Rapacious attention to past content, mannerist form, and the articulation of inarticulate anxiousness – Schnabel's sense 'that things aren't right' – are apocalyptic indicators: they are the constituents of Schnabel's apocalyptic outlook. To have the complete apocalyptic story, we must add his flamboyant theatricality. Indeed, the apocalypse is grand eschatological theatre. Schnabel stages apocalyptic ambivalence with all the theatrical skill he can muster. Out of control, ambivalence seems an omen of impotence and fraught with the danger of arbitrariness. But theatricalised, especially with mannerist cunning, ambivalence becomes a spectacle of heroic openness, generating wildly varied possibilities. Ambivalence can be turned to profound creative use, as Schnabel does, with his openness to all kinds of imagery, materials, and stylistic modes. Such revolutionary openness, which has not been seen in this century since Picasso and Max Ernst, and today exists as well in Kiefer, is inseparable from the apocalyptic mentality – when it has a grip on itself. For apocalyptic destructiveness – overthrowal of the given world – carries within it the seeds of a fresh reality. Schnabel uses his ambivalence as an opportunity for discovery and exploration, suggesting his ego strength – his power to master complexity. His ability to intimate ambivalence and bring it under artistic control – to manipulate the sense of the uncanny – suggests that he should be called the conquistador as well as showman of the apocalypse.

The rediscovery of the past has been a major motivating force in 80s art not simply in acknowledgement of the past's richness, but because the capital of the future seems exhausted; uncertain and humanly bleak. Indeed, the future has been put off indefinitely, so great is the distrust of it. Only a technological future seems available, which, as has been generally realised, does not necessarily mean a humane future. The difficulty of being human is Schnabel's primary message – one of the reasons he is obsessed with archaic signs of the human, that is, the human at its most extreme and so most fundamental.

It is also one reason Schnabel approaches past art, not to exploit it – to confirm its ruin – but with the awareness that its ideological conflicts and stylistic differences are no longer significant. What counts for Schnabel is the desperate spirit of exploration the pioneers of Modern art shared. This idolisation of the spirit rather than letter of the past is another sign of the apocalyptic outlook the *fin de siècle* situation encourages. (It also precludes academicism.) In this situation the artist is neither leader nor follower, innovator nor epigone, but offers a broad view of everything, in expectation of nothing. The slate is wiped clean, with the chance of a fresh start – or a *cul de sac*.

The apocalyptic outlook is always latent, always lurking in the wings of the psyche, for things are always bad, there is always weariness and a sense of *déja vu* in the air, interrupted by bursts of freshness – the sense that life is new – that quickly subsides. But the apocalyptic outlook erupts, virulently, when life seems old, as at the end of a century, and even more at the end of a millenium, such as confronts us. Such turning points spontaneously evoke doubt and hope, anguish and ambition, a sense of loss and of opportunity, of memory and of change. Turning points are inherently ambivalent – Janus-headed, looking both to the past and the future – but above all they force us to look back to where we have come from, not only to surmise where we may be going, but because, perhaps for the first time, we seem to have some distance from it, some perspective on it.

Schnabel looks backward, with all the poignancy that implies, and to convey the anxiousness of the present. His is neither a use nor abuse of the past, but an attempt to show that its anxiousness persists in the present: that is the real continuity. Schnabel's purpose is to grasp this eternal return of anxiousness. In a sense, like the author of *Ecclesiastes*, he is insisting that 'all is vexation of the spirit'. This is the root of Schnabel's conservativism, or rather, conservationism, and of his so-called Neo-Expressionism.

The moment of conspicuous change demands to be marked, celebrated, underlined; it is a reminder that the human project has come this far, survived in however troubled a way, reached another milestone. As noted, the end of a millenium is an even grander birthday than the turn of a century. It promises more, and it signals a greater defeat – the still unhappy state of world and personal affairs, the tyrannised potential that remains and the miserable actuality that no revolution seems able to overcome. It is a sobering moment, as well as one prone to delusions of grandeur. The apocalyptic moment is a moment of high ambivalence, and Schnabel is its most articulate master, utilising an ironic theatrical mode appropriate to it. His broken crockery, discarded Kabuki backdrops, animal skins, velvet, and well-worn tarpaulins are ironic staging grounds from which to launch his various figural elements – persons, objects, gestures, words, and mythological monsters – for these grounds already carry within them the sense of apocalyptic loss and abandonment. They need nothing added to confirm their apocalyptic character. So that for Schnabel to add a figural element to them is to imply the promise of resurrection implicit in the apocalypse, thus completing its representation. *Resurrection: Albert Finney Meets Malcolm Lowry* makes this transparently clear, as does, in a different way, *A D (Wreath for Tennessee Williams)*, 1983, painted on the occasion of the playwright's death. Schnabel's representation of the apocalypse amounts to participatory theatre subsuming us in the sublimity of death while offering us a glimpse of the new life we just might have. Moreover, the tension between ground and whatever is figured on it suggests the tensions that constitute and structure interiority: Schnabel represents the split apocalyptic/resurrectional psyche itself.

His art, establishing a theatrical equilibrium between the extroverted and introverted, presents the apocalyptic mentality in all its grandeur and intimacy, its complex mix of overt irrationality and covert fatalism. Schnabel communicates the private melancholy as well as the public mania associated with the apocalypse. It is because he can hold fast to this maddening doubleness that the maelstrom of the apocalypse is a fountain of artistic youth for him.

The core of apocalyptic ambivalence involves, in the words of the psycho-analyst D W Winnicott, 'doubt as to the outcome of the struggle between the forces of good and evil, or . . . between the benign and persecutory elements within, and without the personality'.[4] This doubt can be maddening, as I have intimated. Schnabel has in fact said that he wants to make paintings 'as mad as possible'. Madness, I want to suggest, is not only a moment of regression, but of mutation, Schnabel's art renders a kind of regression to the archaic in order to mutate the suffering self. In my opinion the moment of mutation is Schnabel's major theme: it is the moment of uncertain resurrection, in which life and death hang in the balance. Sometimes the mutation seems instantaneous, sometimes it seems a slow process. But always there is this moment of organic mutation, suggesting the unexpected generation of unpredictable new life, experienced neither as good nor bad but as radically different.

Mutants pervade Schnabel's work, from *Mutant King* and God in the *Portrait of God,* both 1981, to the creatures in *Fresh Eggs (For Alexander Achilles McEvilley)* and *The Idiot,* both 1985. It should be noted that *Fresh Eggs* commemorates the critic Thomas McEvilley's dead son. It suggests that he has not so much died as mutated, the 'fresh eggs' of the DNZ strip to the right implying a re-birth in unknown new form – a new genesis. This genetic strip recurs in various mutant forms of its own, such as the relatively amorphic black columnar forms flanking *The Idiot.* They have the shape of life but seem dead. Indeed, the recurrent amorphic 'imagery' in Schnabel's pictures suggests the mutational process, the passage through death to unpredictable new life. *Rest,* 1982, commemorates mutation for itself. Sometimes the heart – shown as a combination of bodily organ and machine, as in *Avoiding Open Heart Surgery (Chest Cavity),* 1985 – as well as the stylised genetic material, is used to convey mutation.

Schnabel sets things in mutational flux, which indeed is what the apocalypse does. One sometimes thinks that his work 'illustrates', however loosely, an ancient book of the dead. He seems to believe in a kind of metempsychotic reconception of things, as though everything was 'biodegradable' into art, through which it would reconstitute in sacred new form. The passage through – mutation into – art may be the true passage through death. One may recall that according to metempsychotic 'theory' – fantasy – one is reborn until one is 'enlightened', when one is liberated from the suffering of existence. Also, the less suffering one causes – the less one persecutes or hurts other creatures – the more likely one is to be reborn as a god. Whether *Fouffi-Nouti in Hell,* 1980, or *Maria Callas,* 1982, (four works) – paintings of spirits in passage, like many of Schnabel's figural works – or the broken crockery itself, in all its strangely vital concreteness, Schnabel's work is about beings and things in apocalyptic passage through hell towards a heaven that is unlikely to be there, except in art.

Notes

1 All of these works deal with death and inconclusive transfiguration. For example, the *King of the Wood,* described in Frazier's *The Golden Bough,* is the strongest man of the tribe. The sacred repository of its well-being, he lives in a temple, enjoying the best of everything in life, until he is killed by a competitor, who then takes his place, preserving the strength of the tribe at its optimum. *Resurrection: Albert Finney Meets Malcolm Lowry* alludes to the character who played the long suffering, alcoholic, finally suicidal hero of Malcolm Lowry's extraordinary novel *Under the Volcano,* in the movie of that name made by John Huston. Both heroic figures are suicidal romantic types, manic and melancholic. The psycho-analyst D W Winnicott regards mania as a defence against annihilative tendencies and the awareness of 'death, chaos, mystery' – so evident in Schnabel's works, along with the mania. See D W Winnicott, 'The Manic Defence', *Collected Papers, Through Paedicatrics to Psycho-Analysis,* Tavistock Publications, London, 1958, p 132.

2 Thomas McEvilley, 'The Case of Julian Schnabel' *Julian Schnabel: Paintings 1975-1987,* Whitechapel Art Gallery, exhibition catalogue, London, pp 14-7, documents Schnabel's art-historical sources.

3 A Hauser, *Mannerism, The Crisis of the Renaissance and the Origin of Modern Art,* Routledge & Kegan Paul, London, 1965, pp 24-5.

4 D W Winnicott, 'Psycho-analysis and the Sense of Guilt', *The Maturational Processes and the Facilitating Environment,* International Universities Press, New York, 1965, p 25.

Julian Schnabel, *The Afflicted Organ,* 1987, oil, gesso, mirror on tarpaulin with banner, 320 x 47 cm, courtesy Pace Gallery

Knights in Nights, 1988, oil, 274.3 x 182.9 cm

NEO-TWILIGHT : ROSS BLECKNER

Robert Storr

L to R: *Ellipse of Us*, 1988, oil, 274.3 x 182.9 cm; *Mantle*, 1988, oil, 274.3 x 182.9 cm

To each generation its own decadence. And to each a new dandy. A spleenetic shaman interceding on behalf of the public as much as acting on his own, the dandy of the moment must invent from the complex play of opposites a style that will at once highlight and render bearable the inherent contradictions of our nature and circumstance. 'Looks' count, surface is substance. It is not a casual affair. Dedication to fashion, like other forms of obsession, exceeds merely being 'fashionable,' requiring, as it does, the kind of rigour that most of us fail to bring to any aspect of our lives. Why, then, be disdainful of those who display such discipline, however wilful their artifice. For in laughing at or righteously decrying artifice we do nothing more than expose ourselves as being what Bàudelaire described as '*des gens grave sans vrai gravité*'; in a word, 'dullards.'

In our era, of course, the decadent has become an increasingly difficult role to play, in direct proportion to our familiarity with historical precedents. After all, the dandy as Baudelaire describes him is the incarnation of the singular personality, the 'self-made man' of manners. To fulfill that destiny he must, therefore, abhor even the clichés of his own lineage; from Beau Brummel's cravat and Oscar Wilde's cape to any other already familiar affectation. This said, nevertheless, the decadent sensibility has always been defined by a contradictory awareness of time, a predisposition to remembrance or repetition alternating with desperate longing for immediate sensation. Responding to this combined craving for nostalgia and thrills, decadent style calls for a bit of old and a bit of new, an obsession with 'ruins' mixed with an instinct for the 'latest'. Warhol's answer – as revealed in his posthumous mega-garage sale – was to make the new and collect the old; in his townhouse, Pop pictures thus hung amidst *ancien régime* furniture, a solution presently being reiterated in virtually every interior design magazine.

The supreme dandy of his day, Warhol is still the man to beat. Taste-maker *d'outre-tombe*, in America at least, he has become the most influential artist of his time – for a second time. Unlike Jean-Michel Basquiat, the team of David McDermott and Peter McGough, and other conspicuous members of the Warhol entourage who basked in the reflected black-light of Andy's glory, Ross Bleckner, one of his principal aesthetic heirs, spent the 80s hanging around Julian Schnabel and Barbara Kruger, a range of social loyalties which nicely defines the oxymoronic halves of Bleckner's temperament. Schnabel, self-confessed 'master', pastiches the old; Kruger, severe headmistress of the anti-mastery academy, parodies and deconstructs the Modern. Bleckner, the clever gadfly, does both. The Husymans of contemporary painting in his funereal interiors and still-lifes, Bleckner is at the same time the Eminence-rose of Neo-Geo. His fuzzy stripe paintings of the early 1970s are obvious antecedents of Philip Taaffe's experimental hybrids of high-style Modernism, Newman's 'zip' and Kelly's 'slices', with low-style decorative motifs lifted from grill-work and terrazzo flooring. So too, Bleckner's appropriative experiments can be found reflected in Peter Schuyff's soft-focus Vasarely's and Peter Halley's day-glo Judd's. A dubious legacy perhaps, except that Bleckner's work is lurid fun where that of his epigones is sophomoric or didactic. Consider, for example, Bleckner's huge eye-smarting stripe painting in the form of an heraldic eschuteon, the subliminal message of which flickers like words on the screen of an expiring TV or the text of an Ed Ruscha picture; it reads 'Remember me'. Or take a similar rectangular painting this time framed in floral border of humid reds and greens. Bridget Riley, as a Victorian carpet, Daniel Buren as 'Camp'.

Simultaneously, in what amounts to a kind of aesthetic cross-

Examined Life, 1988, oil, 243.8 x 182.9 cm

dressing, Bleckner makes and shows paintings of a pronounced and haunting romanticism. Beginning with modest atmospheric works – quasi-abstract depictions of the shapes made by streetlights or moonshine falling on nocturnal waters – these pictures evolved into elaborate still-lifes and views of what appear to be the lobbies of opera houses or the vestibule of a private 18th-century mansion. Painted in layers of dark glassy pigments illuminated by impasto nipples in putrescent hues and wraith-like forms in ivory-white these pictures emit a bleak but mesmerising light. More than the sum of their effects, these paintings project an aura at once elegant and repulsive. Where Schnabel's 'grandeur' is constantly betrayed by his provincial-theatre hamming, Bleckner demonstrates a sophistication that is convincing by virtue of its very contrivance.

Decadence bespeaks disillusionment, which in turn presumes prior conviction to some form of ideal. 19th-century decadents were hurt or disabused romantics. Judging from his most recent dark pictures and from the increased proportion of his output which they occupy, Bleckner would appear to be something similar, less a 'Post' than a Late-Modernist. Thus he will say, 'My paintings flirt with belief, both undermining it and establishing it . . . The 20th-century trend has been to empty out assumptions about art and the making of art. Ad Reinhardt for example, is the quintessential deconstructionist in painting; he certainly emptied out abstraction. Duchamp did the same thing in more conceptual work. The irony of emptying out is that things shine with a maximum brilliance just before they die'. He is right, of course. But as accurate or telling as his assessment of Reinhardt is, equally significant is the tone, or rather the echo of his words, recalling as they do those of Baudelaire who wrote, 'Le dandysme est un soleil couchant; comme l'astre qui decline, il est superbe, sans chaleur et plein de melancholie'.

Alas Bleckner has shown himself susceptible to the current vogue for 'philo-speak', mimicking the catch phrases of Post-Modern theory favoured by some of his friends. Without their gift for cold-blooded rhetorical coyness, the words ring hollow in his mouth; for example, '. . . we enter into a symbolic order which is a systematised network of cultural codes and representations which pre-exist, speak or produce an individual subject'. Or 'History needs to be undermined; that's why cynicism is good'. The later remark, be it noted, is closer to Wilde than to Foucault, Lacan or Derrida. Indeed, to re-read Wilde's dialogue 'The Critic as Artist', is to hear the basic tenets of Post-Modernist literary criticism – reading as writing, the elusiveness of the subject – issue forth as Edwardian *bon mots*. Further, it is yet another reason to suspect that the 'Post-Modern' is in essence a once flamboyant Modernism dressed up – or rather down – in dull academic garb.

Alarming only to the most straight-faced of humanists, remarks such as Bleckner's might even be amusing were not so much in the way of art-world success riding on it. In the context of the hard cash economy of 'sighs', such pretence at resistance to the tyranny of cultural representations becomes more than a little suspect. Individuals may be the product of social codes, as Bleckner claims, but certain individuals manage to hoard a disproportionate amount of the surplus 'signifiers' available to 'cultural production'. A freshly minted painting by Bleckner, the latest darling of the market, recently fetched $190,000 at auction. Price does not, of course, discredit a work, but participation in the market on a certain level can, as it has with Kruger, expose a certain logical disingenuousness. In Bleckner's case, the recourse to 'correct' political jargon is altogether beside the point, rather as if Cocteau the fantasist had suddenly felt obligated to speak in the language of Sartre the pamphleteer.

All this belongs however to the annals of art world folly, which at best are a temporary diversion and at worst the affair of those who specialise in grudges. Meanwhile, as Bleckner has said, 'things shine with maximum brilliance just before they die'. All around us now not things but people are dying. To these deaths, Bleckner has dedicated a series of sombre pictures in his neo-romantic mode. *16, 301 + as of January 1987* tells the tale most succinctly, enumerating in its title the number of deaths from AIDS in the United States as of the date it was painted. In America over the past several years we have seen the beginnings of what will no doubt be a flood of art prompted by the onset of this plague. So far much of this work has taken the form of naturalistic theatre and performance art or documentary film and photography. As with any disaster, even those of us who have witnessed it first hand may have difficulty registering what they have seen, and for many who have not the 'facts' must begin their education. 'Realism' thus predominates. Bleckner's pictures constitute a wholly different response; at once a lament and an act of defiance. Using images of an almost frivolous triteness (loving cups and urns surrounded by commemorative ribbons) to a serious purpose, Bleckner's *momento moris* partake of a manifestly fey aesthetic that makes no concessions to 'majority' taste. By thus refusing the restraints so often imposed on the gay community when called upon to represent itself to the public at large, Bleckner's work assumes a genuine political stance. In the context of governmental neglect, general ignorance and social opprobrium, Bleckner's paintings, like the photographs of Robert Mapplethorpe (who appeared at the opening of his Whitney Museum retrospective deathly ill but sporting in a red satin jacket and an ebony and silver capped cane), show the courage of the dandy, the pride that style gives in the face of catastrophe.

'The smell of paint is great but it doesn't make meaning', Bleckner has said. He is right of course. Certainly the sharp contrast between the two halves of his work underscores a profound ambivalence about the seductions of the medium as well as the artist's belief. For the last few years the fascination of Bleckner's work has derived from the friction generated by this self-consciousness exercise in dualism. In the aftermath of Neo-Expressionism, it is the conceptual sides of this equation that has proved most timely. The stripe pictures account for his reputation. Ultimately, it is his murky lightscapes and mournful *vanitas* pictures, the most painterly of his paintings, that place the greatest emotional and intellectual demands on the public. The former show off a dandy's wit, the latter reveal his soul.

Notes

All quotations from Ross Bleckner are from one of eight interviews conducted and edited by Lilly Wei and published as 'Talking Abstract' in *Art in America*, July 1987, p 84. All quotations from Bauderlaire are from 'Le peintre de la vie moderne'.

Andy Warhol, *Twenty Jackies*, 1964, acrylic and liquitex, screenprint, 204.5 x 204.5 cm

AN ACADEMY OF KITSCH

Hilton Kramer

They are as sick that surfeit with too much, as they that starve with nothing – ***The Merchant of Venice***

Jeff Koons, *Travel Bar*, 1986, cast stainless steel, 35.5 x 50.1 x 30.5 cm

The situation in the New York art world at the end of the 1980s is an extremely odd one, for it is a situation that is best comprehended under the rubric of *more is less*. There have never been as many art galleries, as many art museums, as many art exhibitions, as many artists, and as many people spending as much money on art, as we now have. There have never been as many words written about art and artists and the art market. There has never been as much talk about art – though most of the talk is, of course, about reputations and investments and not really about the art itself. There is indeed, more and more of everything – except alas, the one thing that matters most, which is art of genuine aesthetic quality. Since art of real quality is, if anything, in even shorter supply than usual, the very notion of quality in art has been discarded. To believe in quality would, for one thing, depress the booming art market and for another, deprive a lot of people of their fun. It might even put the prestige of art at some risk. So the concept of quality which requires us to make judgements about art, has been consigned to the dustbin of history. It is now considered a hateful relic of the bad old days when Modernism was ascendant and criticism prided itself on making distinctions. In the Post-Modernist saturnalia that is now upon us, such distinctions are neither possible nor desirable. And so we have more and more of what, from the point of view of aesthetic quality, amounts to less and less.

Still, in order for production and consumption to be maintained in this expanding art economy, ideas of some sort – or if not ideas exactly, then some assertions of the intellect that may be mistaken for ideas – are clearly necessary. After all, even the many people in the art world who can be said to have more money than either brains or taste or sensibility need to be made to feel that they are supporting something significant. Where aesthetic quality is no longer an issue, significance depends on such 'ideas' – which is to say, on some modish cultural programme. The preferred 'idea' of the moment is one that accords to the materials of popular culture – the so-called media arts – a special artistic status. Thus art that either resembles or draws its inspiration and imagery from consumer advertising, television, rock videos, movies, comic strips, and the iconography of politics is more in vogue than ever.

The reasons for this are anything but obscure. Art of this persuasion is guaranteed to elicit an immediate response. It is nothing if not accessible. It doesn't require us to have any knowledge or understanding of previous art. It doesn't in fact, require us to know – or feel – much of anything, beyond the routines of media culture and commercial consumption. All of the emotions it invokes are already known, all of the associations it traffics in are familiar, all of its symbols are commonplace and recognisable. All of the distinctions that once separated the achievements of high art from the commercial vulgarities of popular culture are effectively eliminated, and minds besotted with the easy emotions and numbing sensations of the latter are assured of encountering no obstacles in coming to terms with the debased objects that are now offered *as* high are. Everything that was difficult and daunting about the classic productions of Modernist art – above all, its challenges to the eye and the intellect and the emotions – has been expunged in favour of a mode of visual discourse that flatters the lowest taste.

Is it any wonder then, that in this dismal situation, in which kitsch is king, the late Andy Warhol should emerge – or rather, re-emerge posthumously – as the most admired and exalted artist of our time? The recent Warhol retrospective at The Museum of Modern Art was in this respect, an event of really shattering importance. One of the ideas it shattered was the conviction that this museum, which some of us still believe to be the greatest of its kind in the world, would any longer stand for what its name signifies. We were notified that henceforth MoMA would become an important branch, if not indeed the headquarters, of that academy of kitsch that now rules the New

Jeff Koons, *Rabbit*, 1986, cast stainless steel, 104 x 48.3 x 30.5 cm

York art scene with an imperious commercial swagger.

With the sole exception of the mammoth Picasso retrospective, which in 1980 filled the entire museum, the Warhol show was the single biggest exhibition that MoMA had devoted to an individaul artist since it opened its doors in 1929. And almost as important as the show itself was the special Warhol boutique that MoMA set up off the main lobby – an emporium where at every hour of the day starry-eyed consumers could be seen standing in line at the cash registers with shopping carts overflowing with the incredible array of books, catalogues, albums, posters, and other memorabilia that now pour off the press in an unending stream. Warhol had once said that he thought department stores were rather like museums, and MoMA took the hint by transforming itself for the occasion into something very much resembling a department store or a supermarket. All thought of aesthetic experience – never mind aesthetic quality – was conspicuous by its absence. We were smack at the centre of that brave new world in which art had been effectively and triumphantly separated from all aesthetic considerations.

The reception accorded the Warhol retrospective was only another sign of how far things had gone. It came as no surprise that Warhol would be acclaimed as a master in the world of fashion, for that was the world he had come from as a commercial illustrator. Nor could anyone be shocked by the attention lavished upon the show by the media, for he was after all, very much their offspring. What this new development in the art world requires for complete success however, is an unholy alliance between the arbiters of chic and the exponents of academic opinion; the one providing the requisite component of glamour, the other supplying some simulacrum of disinterested ratiocination. For the latter, MoMA recruited two well-known professors – Robert Rosenblum and Benjamin H D Buchloh – to contribute the appropriate encomia to its glossy, expensive catalogue. But even these eager academic acolytes were outdone by the Johnsonian Professor of Philosophy at Columbia University – Arthur Danto – who, in his capacity as the art critic of *The Nation*, disclosed that Warhol was 'to my mind the nearest thing to a philosophical genius the history of art has produced'. Could there any longer be any question but that we had entered a new period?

The stars of this new period, following in the wake of the Warhol ethos, are obliged of course, to introduce certain modifications and alterations in the ways they exploit the current taste for kitsch. One way, best exemplified by the phenomenal success of Jeff Koons, is to plunge art ever more deeply into the bottomless pit of sheer tastelessness. With its vast production of debased artifacts, popular culture can be counted upon to turn up an endless supply of models for an artist of Koons' persuasion to emulate and embellish. The trick I suppose, is to select precisely the model that is guaranteed at the moment to cause the requisite shudder – a shudder of pleasure for those who have surrendered to the Warhol ethos, and a shudder of pain for those who have not. Koons found such a model in the kind of dumb porcelain figurines that are still mass-produced on a gigantic scale in every industrialised nation in the world – objects that might be said to be the quintessential kitsch artifacts. By enlarging the scale of such an object to that of a life-size, free-standing sculpture, and then combining it with an icon of popular culture, Koons produced – or rather, had produced for him by experienced artisans in Italy – the work called *Michael Jackson and Bubbles*. This set a new standard, which is to say a new low, for the academy of kitsch. Need one add that in a very short time Koons has become a very rich man and a new art-world celebrity as the result of this ghastly triumph? One cannot be confident that this new low in tastelessness will not be soon eclipsed by further plunges into the pit, but for the moment Koons remains unrivalled as Warhol's pre-eminent successor.

Another way to exploit the new taste for kitsch-as-art is to eschew the avowedly cynical course of an artist like Koons in favour of something more ponderous and political. This is what we are given in the so-called 'word art' of Jenny Holzer. The particular genre of popular culture she draws upon is the kind of public electronic signboard most often used in advertising displays and theatre marquees. To this medium Holzer brings an endless stock of dreary feminist complaints, which are abridged into brief phrases and sentences that are flashed with numbing repetition on signboards of various sizes. Lately she has extended her range, so to speak, by moving into a more marketable medium – a series of marble coffins, which the artist prefers to call 'sarcophagi', on the surfaces of which are the handsomely carved words (carved by some expert stone-carver) which rehearse at greater length the same repertory of feminist *Laments*, Holzer's title for this series. It will convey something of the emotional tenor of these *Laments* perhaps, to learn that Holzer's most vocal champion – Kay Larson, the art critic of *New York* magazine – has described them as 'dull and changeless as death'. This I believe, contributes something new to the lexicon of critical praise, and we have the academy of kitsch to thank for that too.

Should it come as a surprise to be told that Jenny Holzer has been selected as the artist to represent the United States at next year's Venice Biennale? Not really. As a votary of the new kitsch-as-art school, she is right in the mainstream of the prevailing fashion, and the feminist component of her work adds just the kind of political spice that is also very much in favour just now.

It may help to put this historic apotheosis of kitsch into perspective to be reminded of the classic essay which the American critic Clement Greenberg wrote on this subject exactly 50 years ago. In 'Avant-garde and Kitsch', which first appeared in *Partisan Review* in 1939 and was then reprinted in Cyril Conolly's *Horizon* in 1940, Mr Greenberg was concerned to distinguish between the genuine achievements of Modernist art which it was then still possible to characterise as avant-garde, and this other realm of culture to which, as he said, 'the Germans give the wonderful name of *kitsch* '. 'Where there is an avant-garde', he wrote, 'generally we also find a rear-guard', and he described the latter as 'etsatz culture . . . destined for those who, insensitive to the values of genuine culture, are hungry nevertheless for the diversion that only culture of some sort can provide'.

In describing kitsch moreover, Mr Greenberg gave us an account of a phenomenon that we easily recognise today in the new academic art. In fact he described it – in words that have acquired a special resonance with the passage of time – *as* a form of academic art. 'Kitsch', he wrote, 'uses for raw materials the debased and academicised simulacra of genuine culture'. And further : 'Kitsch is mechanical and operates by formulas. Kitsch is vicarious experience and faked sensations. Kitsch changes according to style, but remains the same. Kitsch is the epitome of all that is spurious in the life of the times. Kitsch pretends to demand nothing of its customers except their money – not even their time'.

'Self-evidently', Mr Greenberg added, 'all kitsch is academic; and conversely, all that's academic is kitsch. For what is called the academic as such no longer has an independent existence, but has become the stuffed-shirt "front" for kitsch.'

Reading this passage, it is worth recalling that it was Andy Warhol who in the 1960s was one of the people who led the revival of 19th-century academic painting and created the vogue for the most aesthetically woebegone Salon painting that is still with us. In its origin I assume, this revival of academic trash began as a Camp gesture, but what began as Camp very quickly acquired a mainstream respectability. The advent of Pop Art in the early 60s had brought into the art world among much else, a whole new public – a public that was fundamentally philistine in its culture and therefore found Modernist art too difficult, too hermetic, too intellectually taxing. This is the public that has now expanded to such a scale that it has even taken possession of the museums that were once notable for resisting it. And this needless to say, is the public that has embraced the new academy of kitsch with such enthusiasm.

It has been aided in its expansion, both in numbers and in influence, by the disappearance of anything that can legitimately be described as

Jenny Holzer, from the *Survival* Series, 1987, installation in San Francisco

avant-garde. By my historical reckoning, the Abstract-Expressionist movement of the 1940s and 50s was the last that could be seriously described as avant-garde. What happened in the 60s was the appropriation by Pop Art of the gestures of the old avant-garde – its air of shock and scandal etc – without any of the content that made the avant-garde a genuine aesthetic force. From the 1960s onwards, what remained authentically Modernist in art could no longer be considered avant-garde, and what called itself avant-garde was likely to be one or another species of academic kitsch.

There is a direct relationship moreover, between the way the art world had expanded in recent years – this horrible phenomenon of more and more of everything but the genuine article – and the domination of kitsch that is now such an established datum of the New York art scene. As the numbers of everything have increased, it is not only art of genuine quality that has declined. So has the public for such art. The revenge of the philistines has been triumphant and meretricious; low-taste art of the kind produced by Warhol and his heirs – among whom Jeff Koons and Jenny Holzer are particularly conspicuous – has been rewarded on a scale reminiscent of the bogus success enjoyed by the official Salon artist of the 19th-century. It is no accident, as they say, that the same academics who are nowadays unstinting in their praise for Warhol, Professor Rosenblum for example, have also been active in re-habilitating the reputations of the worst hacks of the last century, according them positions of artistic parity with the greatest of the Modernist masters who were their enemies.

Next year, just a bit over half a century since Clement Greenberg wrote 'Avant-garde and Kitsch', the Museum of Modern Art will put its seal of approval on this great reversal of taste and standards with a huge exhibition to be called 'High and Low', a show that is said to be a survey of the high Modernist art the MoMA was founded to celebrate and preserve, and the kitsch that is now discovered to be a 'source' of that art; It is a pity that the curators responsible for this show don't have the courage to call it 'Avant-garde and Kitsch'. That way we would be given a more vivid sense of the surrender – a surrender to the academy of kitsch – that the idea of the show represents.

Notes

Hilton Kramer is editor of *The New Criterion*, a monthly review, and art critic of *The New York Observer*. He is the author of *The Age of Avant-Garde* and *The Revenge of the Philistines*, both published by Secker & Warburg.

Jenny Holzer *Above*: from the *Survival* series, 1983, unex sign, 77 cm x 2.8 m x 30.5 cm; *Below*: *Under a Rock Ed 6*, 1986, eletronic indication panel, 14 x 117 cm

BRUCE NAUMAN
Neon Works

Life Death/Knows Doesn't Know, 1983, neon tubing with clear glass, suspension glass, 203.2 and 273 x 271.8 cm

Since the late 50s, and the work of Andy Warhol, Roy Lichtenstein, Tom Wesselman and James Rosenquist, artists have appropriated the medium of advertising, not only as a means of experimenting with new materials in an abstract sense, but as a means of instant communication, of conveying messages and statements (often with socio-political content) through a visual sign language, and of transforming a commercial, consumer language into the context of fine art.

Bruce Nauman began incorporating neon (coloured-glass illuminated tubing) into his multi-media art in the mid-60s, as a medium for abstraction; but soon became concerned with the idea of communicating meaning: '. . . I wanted to get away from what appeared to be abstract, formal sculpture . . .' He came to conceive of his neons in terms of visual signs rather than sculptures, recognising the potential of the advertising medium for social and political commentary:

> I had an idea that I could make art that would kind of disappear – an art that was supposed to not quite look like art. In that case, you wouldn't really notice it until you paid attention. Then, when you read it, you would have to think about it.

It is significant that Nauman sees his art, which explores light and spatial boundaries through the effects of neon light, in terms of *reading signs* rather than merely looking at colours and forms, forcing the viewer to go beyond the initial surface impact of the medium. His neons confront the meaning of language, and indeed much of his art concerns the ambiguous function of language as a means of communication, inspired by his readings of Wittgenstein.

For Nauman, words are as much visual as vocal, and language – in terms of signs and symbols – is the essential medium of communication. Nauman's neons confront the viewer in a direct and unambiguous way, through isolated words, letter inversions, poems, simple word play, or more complex messages, examining language and meaning, and forcing a recognition of contemporary issues.

Nauman has responded to criticisms of his art, namely that his neons – signs intended to 'not quite look like art', making socio-political statements through a commercial medium– exist in the context of art galleries rather than public streets:

> That's a problem either way. If you avoid an art-related situation altogether – if you hang a neon sign anyplace – it is ignored and people don't give it any thought at all . . . in the museum setting the seriousness of looking is often very narrow in its perspective. It may leave out much of the information that's most important to the work, aside from formal considerations. But I don't know of any effective way – outside of galleries or museums – to have people pay attention.

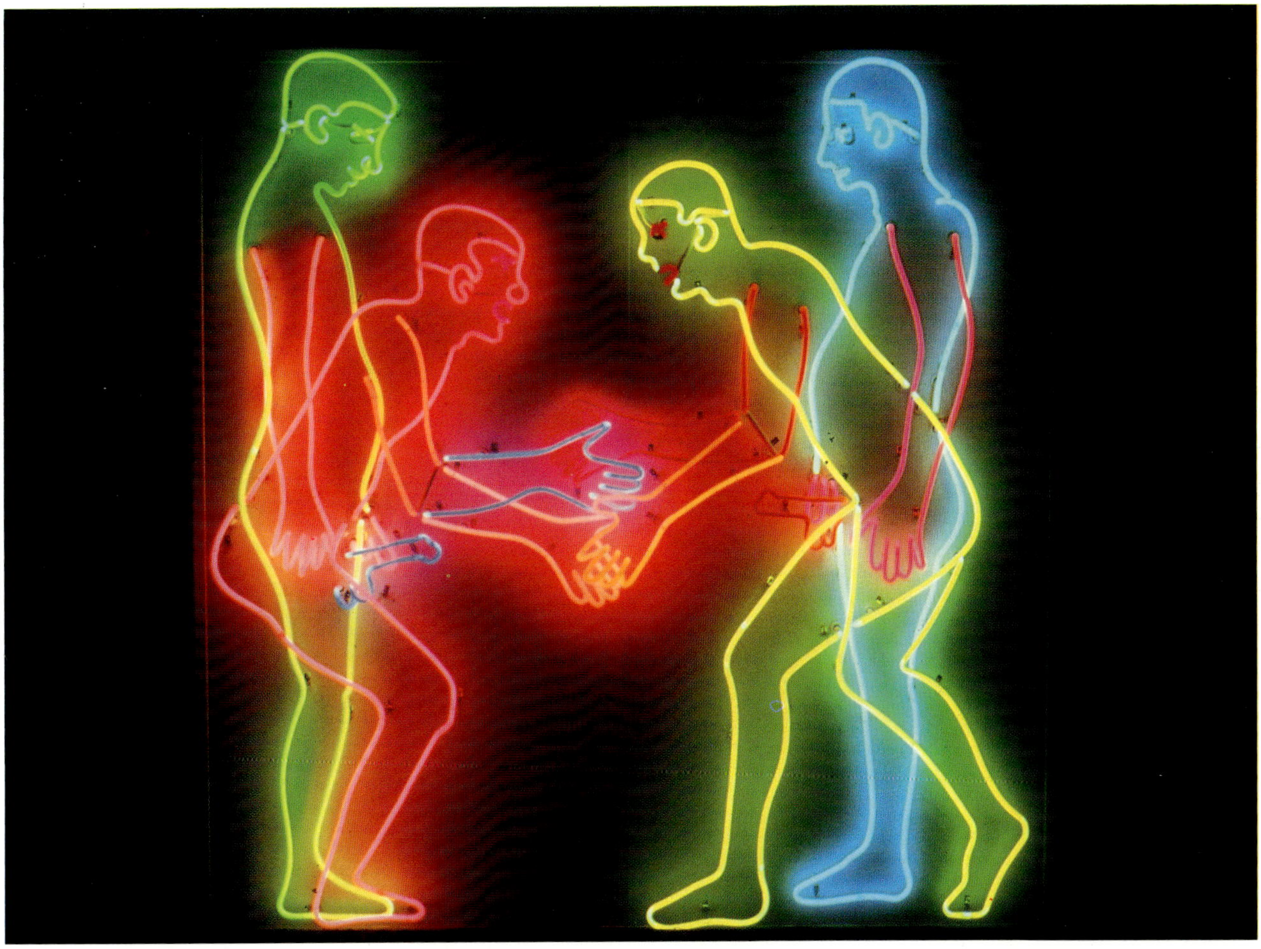

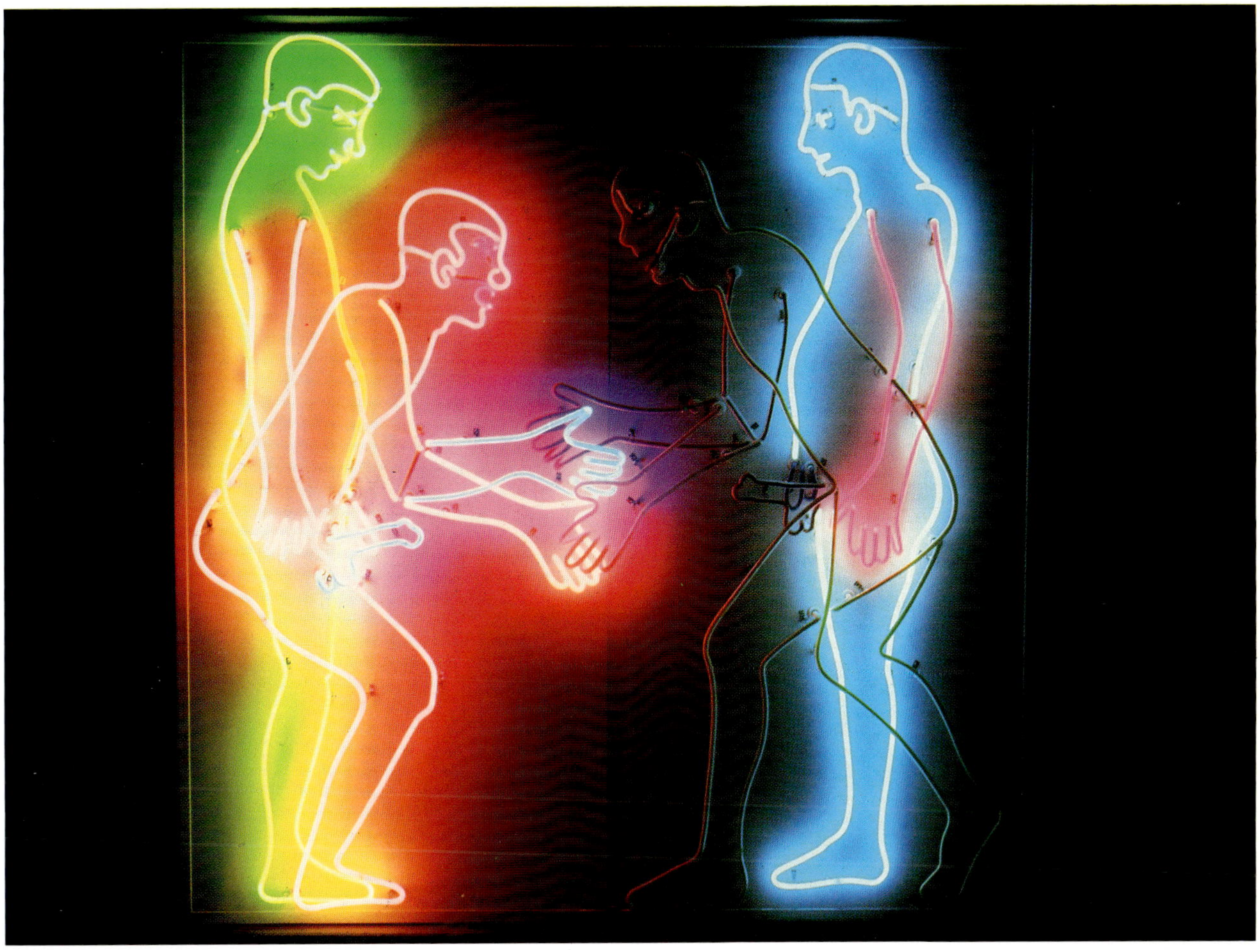

Above and Below: *Welcome Shaking Hands*, 1985, neon and glass tubing, 182.9 x 182.9 x 25.4 cm

Marsden Hartley, *Painting, Number Five*, 1914-15, oil, 100.3 x 80.7 cm. Unusual amongst his contemporaries who visited Europe in the first decades of the 20th century, Hartley made Germany rather than Paris his geographical and aesthetic base. He made contact with members of the Blue Rider such as Franz Marc and Kandinsky, combining Cubist principles with the colour and aesthetics of German Expressionism. On his early trips to Berlin (1913 and 1914-15), he incorporated brightly coloured German military symbols into Cubist formats, producing his most powerful paintings, the *War Motif* series of which this is an example. His work was included in the 1913 Armory Show and played an important part in establishing a place for avant-garde art in America.

AMERICAN ART IN THE 20TH CENTURY

Andrew Causey

George Bellows, *Dempsey and Firpo*, 1924, oil, 129.5 x 160.7 cm. This work was the final expression of the theme of the prize fight which Bellows used between 1907-24 as the subject of six major oil paintings and related drawings and prints.

For many people art begins in the United States with the New York School during the Second World War, while a few familiar names from the earlier years like Georgia O'Keeffe and Edward Hopper are seen as lone stars rather than part of a wider scene. America's ties with Paris following the 1913 Armory Show of modern European art in New York have of course been recognised. But the internationalist view of a single mainline in Western art, passing periodically from one dominant centre to another, has emphasised the moment when hegemony transferred to New York from war-beleagured Paris in 1940. Concentration on a single artistic location at any one time has tended to deny the New York School's affinities with its native roots.

The idea of a main thread in the visual arts has recently come under pressure. The concept of unique hegemony in the visual arts since 1900 belonging to Paris has been questioned by Robert Rosenblum, who identified a 'Northern European' tradition parallel to the French one. This has affected the study of American art of the 1940s and 50s by highlighting, for example, the affinity between New York School painters and the 18th-century idea of the sublime. A counterweight was thus formed to accepted Modernist connections made by Clement Greenberg and others with Paris: specifically with Cubism and the abstract side of Surrealism.

These changing perspectives have cast doubt, not so much on the idea of America inheriting European traditions than on the precise nature of the traditions themselves. But current work is shifting the emphasis, as reassessment of national characteristics begins, focusing in England on artists like Graham Sutherland and the wartime Neo-Romantics, and in America on the interwar period, the Depression and Regionalist painters like Thomas Hart Benton and Grant Wood. This article engages with the argument, recognising that American art has been made under different conditions from European. But what is most interesting is not the separate issues of national characteristics or relationship with Europe, but the way the two have interacted. This admitted, no purpose is served by detaching the 'heroic' period after 1940 from the earlier decades, as if there was no previous history.

Advanced painting in the 1900s meant the bravura Post-Impressionism of the Ash Can painters, so-called because of the backstreet realism of their view of New York city life. Several of the painters, including John Sloan, Everett Shinn and George Bellows, worked as picture journalists providing visual material for newspapers in the days before photo-reproduction became commonplace. Refusing to take their subjects exclusively from the domestic life and activities of the well-off, they developed a feeling for how the city worked, activities on building sites, life in tenements, leisure pastimes in bars and cafés, boxing rings and sports arenas. Significantly, they introduced the urban scene to American art at the peak of post-Civil War economic success, when unrestricted capitalism was supporting huge construction projects, and there seemed to be many reasons for optimism. Painters celebrated the excitement of the prosperous crowded city, but also sometimes glimpsed poverty and alienation behind the glamour. Bellows' canvases spoke up most clearly for the claims of truth to life as superior to finer aesthetic considerations; his broad slashes of paint express the vitality he found in his subjects. The muscular confidence of Bellows' art appealed to those who had faith in the progress of the modern world and, notwithstanding the opposition of the academic old guard, his success was immediate and undisputed. *Both Members of this Club*, of which Bellows said 'I don't know much about boxing, I'm just painting two men trying to kill each other', illuminates

Jackson Pollock, *Autumn Rythm (No 30)*, 1950, oil, 262.5 x 517.5 cm. In 1947 Pollock's mature and radically innovative painting style emerged. He worked from all sides of the composition, dripping and pouring paint onto the canvas, which he placed directly on the floor. In its emphasis on spontaneous gesture, the energetic involvement of the artist's body, and the primacy of paint, Pollock's mature work constitutes perhaps the most avant-garde and influential achievement of the Abstract Expressionists. *Autumn Rhythm* exemplifies the balance between accident and control that he maintained over his technique and, though non-representational, it evokes nature not only in its title, but in the colouring, horizontal orientation and sense of space and ground.

the national myth of a free competitive individualism.

Ash Can realism, modern looking but easily understood, was challenged from the side of advanced art by the more cerebral Modernism of the Stieglitz circle. German educated, Alfred Stieglitz was a professional photographer (in itself something new) and the gallery owner who first introduced Matisse, Picasso and other advanced Parisians to America in the years before 1914. The home-grown artists Stieglitz nurtured included a high proportion of those who were to be the most interesting artists of the interwar years. The majority had travelled to Paris, had experienced the ferment of Modernism at first hand, and returned prepared for more fundamental change than the Ash Can contemplated. John Martin, for example, painted urban scenes, seeing the thrusting forms of buildings and bridges as emblems of the energy of the great city. But his visions were influenced by Italian Futurism and in this sense his pictures were more modern than Bellows'. Painting in water-colour with a delicate touch, Martin avoided the risk of bombast in bravura Ash Can painting.

Unlike the Ash Can painters, the art of the Europe-oriented Modernists was not definable by subject. Martin was also a landscapist and gauged changing natural moods in a similar way to Paul Nash in England. Arthur Dove made elegant landscape abstractions from ideas connected with the farm where he worked for a living at Westport, Connecticut. Georgia O'Keefe's mysterious near-abstract water-colour studies of the effects of light and darkness over the Texas desert point to the mystical side of her approach, while other work, especially her close-ups of flowers unfolding and in bloom, are intense and voluptuous. The painter-photographer Charles Sheeler treated machine and architectural forms in a hard-edged style, in which the realism almost conceals the artist's Cubist origins. Charles Demuth painted cool, elegant designs based on the colonial and modern industrial buildings of his home town of Lancaster, Pennsylvania, and curious allusive portraits of his friends. Demuth's *I saw the Figure 5 in Gold* evokes his friend William Carlos Williams through reference to Williams' poem about the memory of a gold-lettered fire engine seen on a wet New York late afternoon. Marsden Hartley had already been exploring allusive portraiture, using an abstracted Cubist style to represent emblematically, through references to his uniform and medals, an officer friend with whom Hartley had lived in Berlin, and who was killed early in the war.

Willem de Kooning, *Attic*, 1949, oil, enamel and newspaper transfer, 157.2 x 205.7 cm. This painting forms part of the series of energetic black-and-white abstractions which established De Kooning's reputation as a major painter. Although a leading exponent of Abstract Expressionism – the gestural brushwork exemplifying the new visual language – De Kooning refused to abandon representational subject matter – primarily the female figure. References to the human form persist in the symbols of this work, one of his most abstract works. However, his sensuous handling of the paint surface remains characteristic even though his palette is limited. De Kooning constantly revised his paintings, and *Attic* was shown at two different stages of completion.

The art of the Stieglitz circle is too varied to be encapsulated within an easy definition: a certain elegance and refinement, a liking for water-colour and tempera, precise drawing and sharp clear colour are common features. Self-absorption and detachment from public issues are evident, a measure of cynicism when confronted with such contemporary catchphrases as 'The business of America is business'. This is not the world of Bellows, of artistic virtuosity and the celebration of material success. Artists found themselves out of step with materialism and the tendency to isolationism, while at the same time the macho in art was generally discredited by the war. The new group is a loosely-knit avant-garde finding its way in an environment not in its favour, making an art more private than public, more concerned with expressing aesthetic problems than representing life. America had no precedent for an artistic group in which homosexuals, a woman and a Jew practised on equal terms, while the sense of being outsiders to mainstream society contributed to the independent nature of their art.

As a movement the circle evolved its own strain of crystalline Cubism, yet it is very difficult to consider it modern without appreciating that it had allegiance also to the 18th century, to the rational, functional forms of Shaker furniture and the weather-boarded architecture of the north-east. A hero of the movement was Marcel Duchamp without whose presence in New York during the war American art would certainly have been very different. His ironical humour, paradoxical mixture of rationalism and anarchy, his courtesy, charm and self-protective inscrutability, all struck a chord with the American artists, and gained him an impressive following. His belief in the need to 'return art to the service of the mind' stimulated American artists to explore more intellectual alternatives to the social realism represented by the Ash Can, and his critique of his own art – contained in the comment that he wanted to 'return to a completely dry drawing' – helped confirm American painters in their rejection of expressionist gusto.

The depression countered detachment, aestheticism and Europeanism with a revival of national feeling and a search for roots in small-town values at a time when New York, the business centre, was out of favour because of the slump. A revival of urban realism in the work of Kenneth Hayes Miller, Reginald Marsh and the Fourteenth-Street School was an attempt to turn the clock back, but a re-run of the Ash Can without the

Barnett Newman, *Day One*, 1951-2, oil, 335 x 127 cm. 'We are reasserting man's natural desire for the exalted, for a concern with our relationship to the absolute emotions. We do not need the obsolete props of an outmoded and antiquated legend . . . We are freeing ourselves of the impediments of memory, association, nostalgia, legend, myth . . . that have been the devices of Western European painting. Instead of making cathedrals out of Christ, man or "life", we are making it out of ourselves, out of our feelings . . .' This statement supports the development in 1948 of Newman's new format for painting, based on philosophical principles: large-scale expanses of serene unbroken colour which by the early 50s were expanding to a cathedral-like scale as well as format.

Mark Rothko, *Untitled*, 1952, oil, 21.3 x 205.7 cm. 'Abstract art never interested me; I always painted realistically.' (Rothko) '. . . throughout his career, Rothko was wracked by doubts about abstraction . . . he consistently rejected the notion that his classic paintings were abstract, referring to them instead as "realistic", as having "real and specific meaning", and above all as possessed of significant "subjects" . . . What and how, do Rothko's classic paintings signify? I will not accept the artist's protestations that his work is not abstract . . . I am concerned precisely with how abstract art may be coded, how it may communicate and resist communicating.' (from *Mark Rothko: Subjects in Abstraction*, by Anna C Chave, Yale Univ Press, New Haven & London, 1989.)

bullish optimism of the pre-1914 financial climate met no genuine need.

Threat, uncertainty and dislocation were the characteristic emotions of this period and they appear convincingly portrayed in the Surrealist fantasies of Peter Blume, for example, or the louche sexual encounters between sailors and prostitutes in the painting of Paul Cadmus. But the art of the decade is best represented neither by the pretence of the Fourteenth-Street School that nothing had changed since before 1914 nor by the excesses of Surrealism, which was never central to American Modernism; it is seen most typically through the lonely inhabitants of Edward Hopper's canvases. Hopper identifies the feeling of being an outsider that gives rise to voyeurism; his pictures are frequently about watching but not being seen, and the need for contact, often sexual, a need which is always frustrated. Emotionally withdrawn and cold, the pictures do not show domestic settings, there is none of the familiarity and warmth of home. Itinerants live out of suitcases in lonely hotel rooms, and we as spectators are located outside peering in from the darkness; or we watch an all-night cafe from the shadows on the other side of the street, wary and full of presentiment for something undefined, in a world that belongs to dream or to film noir, that is not wholly real. When the sun comes out unease does not disappear; sunbathing in Hopper's painting, as in Hockney's, is a lonely activity in a world of stillness and silence. Unlike the contemporary painters of the rural scene, Hopper was not attempting the nostalgic recovery of a lost past, but facing up to the alienation he saw as the condition of the new, essentially urban life.

Thomas Hart Benton, a mural painter from Kansas City, illustrates best the Depression era's emphasis on the regions as representative of the true America and the revenge of a narrow isolationist populism on Modernism as promoted by Stieglitz, to whom Benton was rancorously opposed. In murals representing American industry and agriculture Benton evokes harmony and the nobility of the work ethic in a way that is over idealised for a period familiar with lynchings and flagrant racial prejudice (the Scottsboro boys, Sacco and Vanzetti). The political conviction of Benton's Mexican contemporary Diego Rivera was rooted in an understanding of his country's history and present situation, and Rivera's painting was enriched by a first-hand study of earlier didactic mural painting sequences on a long study visit in Italy. Benton's fantasies, by contrast, were not grounded in

Cy Twombly, *Untitled*, 1970, oil and crayon, 156.2 x 190.5 cm. Twombly's early drawings and paintings, characterised by tangled masses of dark pencil and crayon lines, show the influence of Motherwell, Shahn and Kline. His move to Rome in 1957 coincided with the emergence of his mature style, combining his early marks with more legible images – words, letters, numbers – and a personal vocabulary of symbols. While these graffiti-like elements imply a reference to mass culture, anticipating Pop Art and Neo-Expressionism, Twombly continued to paint in a loose, flowing, Abstract Expressionist manner. In his later work, colour and line are devoid of representational allusion and pigment is applied directly onto the surface in an action that resembles writing.

reality and were badly painted. Today, when Modernism has again receded and it is widely felt that the great artists and styles of the past are there for contemporary use, Benton asks to be reconsidered. But today's eclectics reach back to earlier traditions with a knowing sophistication, using them to quote from, pastiche, and make the source of something new. Benton was an innocent, passionate to restore simple values in a world that had moved on. Nonetheless he represents a problem that will not go away. In a recent picture-book of highlights from the permanent collection published by the Whitney Museum of American Art, Benton was represented by a painting of a working man and wife at table under a sampler quoting the opening of the twenty-third psalm, 'The Lord is my Shepherd'. In what is broadly a Modernist presentation this quaint morality tale obtrudes, pinpointing the range of sophistication which is wider in the United States than elsewhere.

Grant Wood, working in Cedar Rapids, Iowa, evoked a prosperous, hardworking agricultural America, by means of a decorative stylised toytown kind of construction reminiscent of folk art. *The Midnight Rise of Paul Revere*, a colonial theme, has a bizarre originality and power resulting from the bird's eye view, the almost cartographical layout of the village below, and the theatrical lighting. The unashamed artifice of this strange design in no way implies lack of feeling or sincerity.

Wood was a more complex artist than Benton. His *American Gothic*, showing the grave figure of a farmer standing pitchfork in hand with his wife in front of their well-kept frame house is one of the iconic images of American art, and has stimulated a steady stream of parodists and cartoonists. It is not Wood's only design in which the emotion is so intense and the innocence of the message so difficult for a 20th-century audience to accept at face value that irony seems undeniable. Wood was a devious artist who concealed passions and ambiguities beneath deceptively calm surfaces and simple forms. He is the opposite in this to Benton whose busy, agitated figures, turn out, when scrutinised, to be superficial and lifeless.

When Clement Greenberg published his article 'Avant-garde and Kitsch' in 1939 he was in effect presenting the Europe-oriented East Coast intellectual's riposte to Benton's cheapening of art. In arguing that the industrial revolution had destroyed true popular art, and that the taste of the contemporary masses was for a debased form of high art – Michelangelo simplified and

Ad Reinhardt, *Abstract Painting, Number 33*, 1963, oil, 152.4 x 152.4 cm. One of the most articulate and scholarly artists of his generation, Reinhardt was an important precursor of Minimalism. By the 1960s, he was producing only symmetrical black paintings of which this is an example. Even though other artists had previously made essentially black paintings, none had made it their primary concern to create 'the last painting which anyone can make'. He saw these works as an 'unmanipulated and unmanipulatable, useless, unmarketable, irreducible, unphotographable, unreproducible, inexplicable icon'. However they soon gained acceptance in the New York art world, becoming exemplars of postwar American art.

packaged for mass consumption – Greenberg challenged American art to recover its seriousness. The background to this challenge had a political side. Many American intellectuals opposed to Nazism and with a Marxist allegiance felt betrayed, first, by the inertia of the masses and their failure to bring into being a popular left-wing movement, and, secondly, by Stalinism and the Nazi-Soviet pact. Greenberg was led to conclude that if art could not fulfil a social role on the left, it should withdraw to look after its own domain. This was the justification for the search to replace the figurative art of the 1930s with the abstractions of the New York School. The art for art's sake Modernism of the following decades originated in a desire to withdraw from social commitment that cannot be traced to a single starting point, but was fundamentally conditioned by that sense of betrayal.

There are parallels between what followed, a more modern and abstract art, and the aftermath of the Armory Show in 1913. Then, the war had also had the effect of promoting the European Modernism presented in the Show by engendering a more sceptical attitude among advanced artists to the world of big business, and bringing to the fore the art of the Stieglitz circle with its attachment to a subjective and avant-garde approach rather than a directly socially-reflective art. By 1940 New York's increasingly sophisticated network of dealers and buyers was making the best contemporary European work widely available there, while the exhibition programme of the Museum of Modern art, founded in 1929, was a powerful force for increasing understanding of the European scene. Institutional developments favouring the Europeans helped make New York the magnet that drew so many distinguished artists to America when war broke out. The parallel between the two periods is only a loose one, too much in America had changed between the wars for a situation to repeat itself precisely. But it is clear that on two occasions in the 1920s and 1940s, American artists found themselves out of sympathy with widely held social values and exchanged a demonstrably American art (Ash Can and later Regionalism) for one that was more modern and international.

With the Abstract Expressionism of Pollock and de Kooning and the Colour Field painting of Rothko and Newman, American art in the 1940s and 50s moved for the first time beyond parameters set up in Europe. That eminent Europeans, such as Breton, Ernst, Léger, Masson, Tanguy and Mondrian, in wartime

Frank Stella, *Silverstone*, 1981, mixed media on aluminium and fibre-glass, 268 x 309.9 x 55.9 cm. During the 1960s, Stella came to the fore as one of the most inventive members of the new school of Post-Painterly Abstraction, attempting to negate illusionism by insisting on the inherent flatness of the picture surface. His works from 1970 onwards mark a change in direction with a renewed emphasis on colour, surface and texture, incorporating into his art some of the gestural aspects of Abstract Expressionism that he had avoided during his previous decade of Minimalist painting. This work is one of a series of paintings known as *Circuits* made between 1981-3. They embody Stella's fascination with competition and speed, especially with car-racing.

exile from Paris, played a crucial role is beyond question – Jackson Pollock spoke for many New York painters when he told an interviewer in 1944 that he believed everything important in the art of the past hundred years had taken place in Paris. But factors nearer home such as Mexican mural painting, the existence of an American mural programme in the 1930s as part of Roosevelt's New Deal, and indigenous American art were all important influences. The huge abstracts Pollock was making by the late 1940s with their tangled skeins of paint, De Kooning's contemporary near-abstractions with vestiges of human figures embedded in them, or Rothko's flat planes of shimmering colour, are extreme paintings. The art of Picasso, Miro and Matisse is a staring point, but the end result is quite different. The return of the émigrés to Europe with the war's end left the New York painters on their own in what they felt to be a hostile climate of opinion. The public support for artists established as part of the New Deal had ended with the return to full employment in the war, and the economic and political expansionism of the post-war years struck no chord with artists, many of whom had started on the Marxist left and now felt increasingly turned in on themselves and determined to express their isolation in the most positive and unequivocal way they could.

However radical the Stieglitz artists had been, their art is fully comprehensible within a European context: it has a crafted quality, an elegance, a traditionalism that ultimately ties it to Europe and the spirit of the 18th century in America. New York School painters were prepared to take risks and face uncertainty to escape the hold of this tradition. Pollock denied to his interviewer in 1944 that he wanted to create an American painting, declaring (a little illogically) that the very idea was as absurd as an American physics or mathematics. Modernism has been sustained by this remark because it lends weight to the thesis that the new American art was the successor to European. But the remark has been read out of context. As a former pupil and friend of Benton, whose plea for specifically American character was held in growing disdain in the internationalist mood of the 40s, Pollock almost certainly wanted to distance himself from his former teacher's beliefs. He had always rejected Benton's crude didacticism and now felt increasingly remote from figurative painting altogether. But Pollock was unusual among the New York School painters in being a Westerner and in not coming from a recent immigrant family.

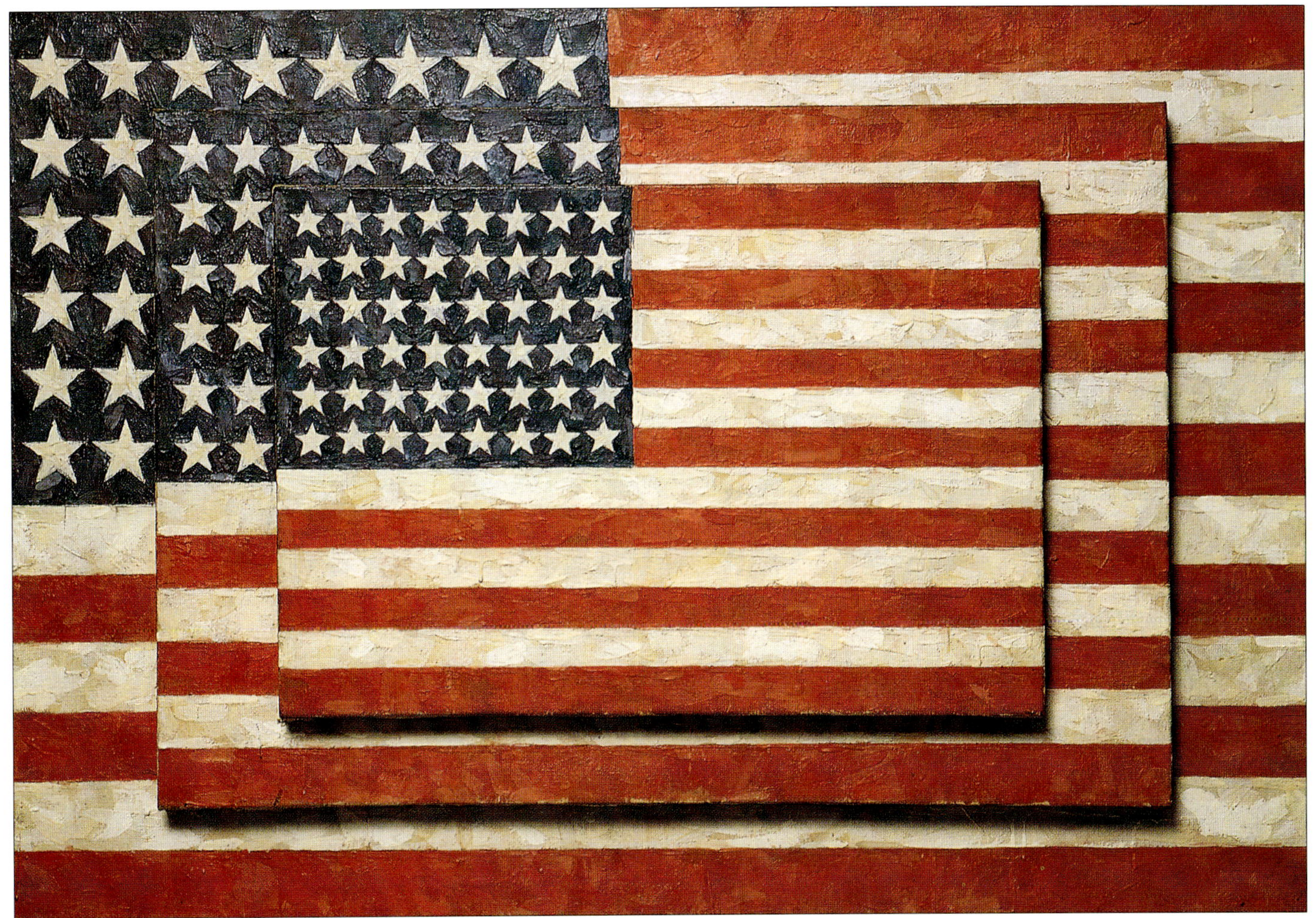

Jasper Johns, *Three Flags*, 1958, encaustic, 78.4 x 115.6 x 12.7 cm. Influenced by the ideas of Robert Rauschenberg and John Cage in the early 50s, the mature work of Jasper Johns began in 1954 with his appropriation of the American flag as his prime pictorial motif. The single flag, and later the target, numbers and the alphabet, became the essential subject matter of his early years. Johns' single flag images never suggest spatial depth, defying the usual pictorial structure of figure against ground. In the tri-levelled *Three Flags*, the culminating work of this first period of Johns' art, the flag subject becomes its own ground. The trio of flags – each one successively diminished in scale by about 25 percent – projects outward, contradicting Classical perspective.

His cultural background was different from that of more educated Jewish colleagues like Newman and Rothko and, unlike them, shared Benton's mistrust of intellectuals and something of his devil-may-care attitudes.

The Abstract Expressionism of Pollock and De Kooning is an art of gesture and spontaneity allowing recall of experience without the intervention of the organising mind: sensations relayed to the canvas with a high measure of discontinuity. It has been a fault of Modernism that, in stressing the avant-garde nature of the New York School and its cohesion as a group, it has tended to erase differences between individual artists. Modernism has favoured abstraction over representation on account of its greater radicalism, and the fact that De Kooning's painting is full of references to life which are often easily legible, while Pollock's is not, is overlooked when the two painters are considered together. They do, of course, have much in common. The multiplicity of marks and gestures within their designs mirrors the speed and intensity with which sensations of movement, light and sound impress themselves on the nerves in a complex environment, which, although they are essentially urban, have, in Pollock's case, rural elements too. The parallels between the artists is evidence that the distinction between figuration and abstraction is not an absolute one.

Where earlier city painters like the Ash Can, have stood outside their subject and described it as spectators, the Abstract Expressionists make it part of themselves. Where Bellows' evocation of the New York cityscape is picturesque and its effect is to romanticise, the Abstract Expressionist makes himself one with the environment. Bellows articulated pride in American achievement, but the Abstract Expressionists' priorities are different; they are not concerned to celebrate urban glamour or modernity like latter-day Futurists, but to convey the essence of their urban experience without the intervention of the banal or familiar image. Their paintings are fragmented and discontinuous, there is nothing tidy or logical about their structures. In this respect Robert Rauschenberg's combine paintings of the 50s, in which the untidy swirls and splashes of paint are embellished with jetsam and urban tat picked off the street, have much in common with De Kooning's art except that with Rauschenberg everyday life is a material part of the picture surface.

Rothko and Newman regarded their paintings, though non-representational, as having subject matter. Newman took the lead

Richard Serra, *Prop*, 1968, sheet: lead antimony, 152.4 x 152.4 cm, pole: lead antimony, 243.8 cm. Serra was one of the 'anti-form' group which gave prominence to unusual techniques and eccentric processes and he was represented in the exhibition arranged by Robert Morris at the Leo Castelli warehouse, New York, in 1968. He worked in a variety of materials, from lead strips, to 16 mm film strip, to hot-rolled steel, the forms dictated by the materials, the process and the force of gravity. The focus on process was continued in his series of Prop sculptures from 1968-70, among which he considered the Whitney example to be 'the generative prop of a series utilising various plates and poles of different dimensions and focusing on the logic of the material under tension'.

James Rosenquist, *House of Fire*, 1981, oil, 198.1 x 542.9 cm. Rosenquist's early career as a bill-board artist is reflected in his use of commercial techniques and materials, his elimination of visible brushwork and in his hard-edged application of paint. From this he developed a method of splicing and combining fragmentary, blown-up images from commercial advertising along with motifs from contemporary culture. In contrast to his earlier paintings, where images were fragmented and overlapped, here the unrelated motifs are presented on individual panels. The allegorical meaning of the work is ambiguous: the brown paper bag turned disconcertingly upside down, the bucket of molten steel, and the barrage of lipsticks hinting at violence, sex, domesticity or war.

Andy Warhol, *Ethel Scull 36 Times*, 1963, synthetic polymer paint silk-screened on canvas, 202.6 x 363.9 cm. Probably the first of Warhol's commissioned portraits, this silk-screened image of Ethel Scull – she and her former husband Robert were in Warhol's own estimation, 'the biggest collectors of Pop Art' of that era – is given the same treatment as the cocoa-cola bottles, in which the serial presentation accentuates the banality of the commercial products. His repeated-image, silk-screen portraits transformed people into products; household names are treated no differently from household goods. The depiction of Mrs Scull in 36 different photo-booth poses was made the same year as his initial activity as a film maker and is appropriately cinematic.

in 1948 in setting up a school which was called 'Subjects of the Artists'. They thought of subject matter not in concrete and physical terms but through existential concepts such as tragedy, anxiety and mystery. In 1947 Rothko spoke passionately against the artists use of conventional subject matter in a society whose values were materialist. 'With us,' he said, 'the disguise must be complete, the familiar identity of things has to be pulverized in order to destroy the finite associations with which our society increasingly enshrines every aspect of our environment.'

In 1949-50 several New York School painters started working on vastly larger canvases, not in order to make didactic paintings, like the Mexicans or Benton, but, paradoxically, to create a private world. Rothko described his purpose in 1951: 'I realise that historically the function of painting large pictures is painting something very grandiose and pompous. The reason I paint them, however – I think it applies to other painters I know – is precisely because I want to be very intimate and human. To paint a small picture is to place yourself outside experience . . . However you paint the large picture you are in it.' Rothko and Newman insisted that their pictures were to be seen not from a distance where the whole could be absorbed in a single view but from close up where the viewer was dwarfed by the canvas. The canvas became like an environment.

It has always been accepted that social alienation was a motive for the New York painters advocacy of an art that was abstract and not easily accessible. The development of Pop Art from the mid-50s was certainly a sign that the retreat of the artist from his audience was over. But the terms on which the common object returned to avant-garde art are not straightforward. Certainly the Pop artist's relationship to the object is not simply one of celebration. Jasper Johns' flags, for example, which were one point of origin for Pop Art, are ambivalent in implication: an image that carries specific cultural connotations is manipulated and transformed as the artist disturbs the naturally flat surface of his subject with impasto on the canvas, adds extra stripes or a blank white area below; he moulds the image not to reassure the observer of its integrity but to create fear for its loss. Johns is a destabilising artist. In the map pictures names of states are switched to locations where they do not belong and names of colours are inscribed over areas of paint of a different colour. Johns threatens identity rather than affirming it.

The realist tradition, of which Pop is a part, has exceptionally strong in America, starting from the late 19th-century *trompe l'oeil* pictures of William Harnett with their brilliant painted simulations of bulletin boards and still life ensembles, through the cubist paintings of Stuart Davis and Gerald Murphy in the 1920s, to Pop and Photo-Realism. The attitude to the objects presented has been ambiguous. The *trompe l'oeil* paintings are saturated with a nostalgia that implies loss. The Cubists confront consumer objects and packaging with unprecedented directness, but even with Stuart Davis there is an emphasis on the particular and the strange rather than the typical (which interested the contemporary Purists in Paris). Similarly the approach of Pop artists is not just a celebration of the object. Warhol's repetitions imply boredom, Lichtenstein's parodies stress cliché, and both artists are interested in sign systems and methods of communication as well as in the objects themselves. Wesselmann's Great American Nudes seem at first to be directly presented and realistic, but their style, reminiscent of Matisse, reminds us that they belong to art as much as life, while their scale and bright simple colours recall billboards, so that they are distanced from us in that sense as well.

20th-century American artists have had a complicated relationship with Europe. They have been drawn by its lure and conscious at the same time of the risk, in pursuing transatlantic modernism, of compromising their native inheritance. Long before cheap air travel, even before the Armory Show, it was normal for ambitious painters to study in Europe. Most of the artists in the Stieglitz circle travelled to Europe when young, then hardly ever, if at all, later. Their sophistication was European, but their feeling for landscape and nature (which has parallels in England but not in France) was connected with the contemplative and pantheistic tradition of Thoreau and Emerson, and marked the tentative, subjective genesis of American scene painting. Similarly, New York school art grew from association with European Modernism, but at the very moment when that contact was bearing fruit the painters seemed most concerned to stress features such as large size, strong emotion, and rawness of finish that might identify their work as specifically American. While Pop Art exemplifies the common identification of America with consumerism, it emerges under scrutiny not as less straightforward than it seems, the directness of its thrust periodically undermined by conceits and ironies that connect it with a European tradition of scepticism and doubt.

Philip Pearlstein, *Female Model on Adirondacks Rocker, Male Model on Floor*, 1980, oil, 182.9 x 182.9 cm. The human form is treated like a still-life: sexually alienated, and psychologically empty, Pearlstein's nude figures are bathed in harsh artificial light.